Date Due

WE CAN FLY

Stories of Katherine Stinson
and Other Gutsy Texas Women

WE CAN FLY

Stories of Katherine Stinson and Other Gutsy Texas Women

by Mary Beth Rogers, Sherry A. Smith and
Janelle D. Scott
drawings by Charles Shaw

Ellen C. Temple • Publisher, Austin, Texas
in cooperation with Texas Foundation for Women's Resources

First Edition
All rights reserved. Printed in the United States of America.

Library of Congress Cataloging in Publication Data

Rogers, Mary Beth.
    We can fly, stories of Katherine Stinson and other gutsy Texas
women.

    Bibliography: p.
    1. Women — Texas — Biography. 2. Stinson, Katherine, 1891–
1977. 3. Women — Texas — History. 4. Texas — History. I. Smith,
Sherry A., 1952–   . II. Scott, Janelle D., 1948–   . III. Title.
HQ1438.T4R63   1983   920.72'09764   82-80441
ISBN 0-936650-02-8
ISBN 0-936650-03-6 (pbk.)

Thanks are due the authors and copyright holders who permitted excerpts from the following works to be included in this book:

This Life I've Led, by Babe Didrikson Zaharias; copyright © 1955.
By permission of George Zaharias.

'Whatta-Gal': The Babe Didrikson Story, by William Oscar
Johnson and Nancy P. Williamson; copyright © 1975. By permission of Little, Brown and Company.

Theatre-in-the-Round, by Margo Jones; copyright © 1951. By permission of Holt, Rinehart and Winston Publishers.

Clara Driscoll: An American Tradition, by Martha Anne Turner;
copyright © 1979. By permission of Martha Anne Turner.

*Black Women Oral History Project Interview With Christia
Adair*, by Dorothy R. Robinson; copyright © 1977. By permission of Schlesinger Library, Radcliffe College.

"Space Cadet," by Lawrence Wright. Reprinted with permission
from the July issue of *Texas Monthly*. Copyright © 1981 by *Texas
Monthly*.

"NASA Picks Six Women Astronauts With the Message: You're
Going A Long Way, Baby," *People* Weekly 2/6/78; copyright
© 1978, Time Inc. By permission of *People* Weekly.

"Sextet for Space," copyright © 1978 by Newsweek Inc. All rights
reserved. Reprinted by permission

Charles Goodnight: Cowman and Plainsman, by J. Evetts Haley;
copyright © 1949. By permission of J. Evetts Haley.

Thanks are due the owners who permitted copies of their
photographs to be used in this book. Credits accompany each
photograph.

Ellen C. Temple–Publisher
Austin, Texas

TABLE OF CONTENTS

PREFACE

WE CAN FLY is an outgrowth of the two-year touring exhibition,
Texas Women — A Celebration of History.

The exhibition, which was created by the Texas Foundation for Women's Resources, featured stories, photographs, artwork and artifacts representing more than 150 outstanding Texas women. However, exhibit formats allow only a few sentences and one or two photographs about each woman. *Texas Women* researchers unearthed mounds of information which simply could not be included in the exhibition. And some of the stories they uncovered are too important to remain untold.

This fact, combined with the knowledge that Texas history students have very little information about any of the women who played significant roles in the social, political, cultural or economic development of Texas, led us to undertake this new project.

When Ellen C. Temple·Publisher proposed to publish a series of books about women in Texas history, the Texas Foundation for Women's Resources agreed to use its *Texas Women* material to compile this collection of stories.

We Can Fly examines the lives of 12 individual women and the composite story of two groups of women — the Flying WASPs of World War II and the Space Women, America's first women astronauts. All except the astronauts were featured briefly in the *Texas Women* exhibition.

Any number of outstanding women — in addition to the ones included in *We Can Fly* — could have been selected. But we chose these particular women because several common threads run throughout their lives:

• *They dared to dream extraordinary dreams.* They wanted to achieve what few people — especially women — had achieved before. They wanted to break new ground, blaze new trails or set new records. They did not have ordinary goals. They wanted something "extra" out of life.

• *They took risks to make their dreams come true.* Sometimes the risks were physical — when Jovita Idar faced down the Texas Rangers, or when the astronauts learned to live with the ever-present danger of death in space training or travel, or when Molly Goodnight lived virtually alone on the prairie. Other times the risks were financial — when Bette Graham tried to set up a new business while worrying about having money to buy groceries, or when Margo Jones set out to raise money for a pioneer theatrical venture few people thought would succeed. And sometimes the risks were emotional — when Jane McCallum endured the ridicule and sarcasm of critics who opposed her efforts to win the right to vote for women.

• *They had an impact on Texas.* Although not all of the women were born in Texas, or even lived here for all of their lives, they did something important or exciting enough here to make Texans sit up and take notice. Katherine Stinson's daring stunt flights helped call public attention to San Antonio's potential as a major aviation center. Although Leonor Villegas de Magnon spent much of her time in Mexico, her volunteer work and writings had a great influence on Texas Mexican-Americans. Margo Jones' theater and Bette Graham's invention contributed to the "can-do" attitude that makes Dallas a leader in business and the arts. And the women astronauts who lived near Houston and trained at the Lyndon B. Johnson Space Center had an impact not only on Texas, but also on the nation.

• *They overcame obstacles and personal disappointment.* Christia Adair, who was black, overcame the discrimination against her and worked for years to chip away at segregation laws and practices in the South. Katherine Stinson had to give up flying because of her health, but went on to another career in architecture. Many of these women, faced with widowhood or divorce, chose to build entirely new lives for themselves, rather than wallow in self-pity or despair.

• *They were persistent.* They would not take no for an answer. Babe Didrikson Zaharias won golf tournaments — even after her cancer had been diagnosed and was sapping her energy. Sofie Herzog practiced medicine *her* way — in spite of the disapproval of Brazoria townspeople who were shocked by her unorthodox behavior. The WASPs worked for more than 30 years to achieve formal recognition for their war-time flight service. Mary Cleave had to wait years and apply twice before she was admitted to the space program.

• *They had unusual self-confidence.* Most of these women believed they were special and that their talents, skills, abilities and judgment would allow them to succeed. Like Katherine Stinson, most said at one time or another, "I believe in myself."

The women featured in *We Can Fly* believed they had something important to do or say. They were very much aware of their ability to influence or shape the course of events and the lives of others. They believed they could — and would — succeed. And with that belief, they let nothing stop them from making their dreams come true.

The Texas Foundation for Women's Resources and Ellen C. Temple·Publisher are proud to present these stories. And we are particularly grateful to the Bette Clair McMurray Foundation, George and Ronya Kozmetsky of the RGK Foundation and Katherine B. Reynolds, whose significant financial support made the development of the manuscript possible.

We Can Fly is based on the Texas Foundation for Women's Resources' files, assembled under the supervision of Research Director Ruthe Winegarten and exhibition researchers Rose Brewer, Evey Chapa, Martha Cotera, Nancy Fleming, Willie Lee Gay, Martha Hartzog, Melissa Hield, Claire Keefe, Merily Keller, Barbara Lau, Patricia Martin, Leatha Miloy, Mary Sanger, Janelle Scott, Sheila Smith, Sherry Smith, and Frieda Werden. Janelle Scott conducted additional research and wrote much of the material in *We Can Fly.* Ellen Jockusch provided research about Babe Didrikson Zaharias and wrote portions of that chapter. Sherry Smith secured all of the photographs and permissions and assisted in the overall editing. Charles Shaw designed and illustrated the book.

The members of the board of directors of the Texas Foundation for Women's Resources, which adopted this project in 1981, have supported it enthusiastically from the beginning. They are Cathy Bonner, Judith Guthrie, Jane Hickie, Katherine B. (Chula) Reynolds, Ann Richards, Martha Smiley, Ellen Temple and Sarah Weddington.

We are grateful to all of these people and to the Friends of the Texas Foundation for Women's Resources.

— Mary Beth Rogers **9**

New Year's Day Celebration
State Fair Grounds---Sacramento---Jan. 1, 1918

KATHERINE STINSON
International Champion Aviatrix

Benefit Sacramento Braves

The years between Orville and Wilbur Wright's first successful airplane flight in 1903 and the United States' entry into World War I in 1917 were exciting times for the early aviation industry. Flying was still a novelty — almost a sport. Enthusiastic crowds gathered at air shows across the nation — just to see if the strange, motor-powered flying machines could get off the ground and stay there! And they admired anyone brave enough to sit in one of the flimsy, open-air planes and try to fly it into the air. The early pilots were as popular as movie stars or sports heroes — and much more daring. Few men were courageous enough to try flying. And it was almost unheard of for a woman to take to the air in a plane.

Young Katherine Stinson did, and some people called her the "world's greatest woman pilot." In 1912, she became the fourth licensed woman pilot in the United States. She began her aviation career 11 years before Charles Lindbergh took his first flying lesson, and 16 years before Amelia Earhart became the first woman to fly solo across the Atlantic. Thousands of people watched Katherine Stinson perform daring stunt flights. Stinson fan clubs sprang up around the world. Katherine Stinson established speed, distance and endurance records, and she helped the early aviation industry gain public acceptance and popularity. This is Katherine Stinson's story.

We Can Fly
KATHERINE STINSON

(1891 – 1977)

She had no plans to become the world's greatest woman pilot.

Originally, all Katherine Stinson wanted was to go to Europe to study music and then to come back to America to be a great piano teacher. However, because her family was not wealthy, Katherine had to earn the money to pay for her trip to Europe.

How was a 19-year-old girl going to earn that much money in 1910? Perhaps she could be a secretary, a teacher or a store clerk. Those were the best jobs women could find then.

"I figured that I'd be about 90 years old before I could save enough in any of those ways, so I decided I'd have to find something else," Katherine said.

Then young Katherine read a newspaper article about the pilots who put on air shows — exhibitions that showed off the newest in airplanes. Pioneer pilots flew daring stunts over vacant fields on the outskirts of towns and cities all over America. They tested their own courage and ability, as well as the endurance of newly developed flying machines. Some of these pilots earned $1,000 a day!

Katherine had an idea. Perhaps this was the way she could earn a lot of money in a very short time. Besides, it looked like fun.

"If other people could do it, so could I," Katherine thought.

First, she had to persuade her parents.

Katherine already knew how to drive a car, something most young women did not do in 1910. Her mother had given her permission to learn, then had served as a contented passenger while Katherine drove around the countryside.

"When I began to talk about flying, she already had confidence in me," Katherine said about her mother.

Convincing her father was more difficult.

"My father didn't approve in the *least*. He was like the hen with an unmanageable duckling in its brood. But I finally gained the consent of both my parents, and . . . I set out to be an aviator — as a means to becoming a music teacher," Katherine said.

Katherine had never flown before. Neither had most Americans. Very few people knew what flying was like. Many were too afraid to try it. But not Katherine.

When she took a hot-air balloon ride with friends in Kansas City in 1911, Katherine found out that riding in the sky was exhilarating. She had a wonderful feeling as she floated peacefully in the air, high above the trees and houses below. What was there to fear?

Now Katherine wanted to ride in one of those new airplanes she had been reading about.

Her friends told her that airplanes were different. After all, hot-air balloons had been around for years. But airplanes! They were noisy and dangerous. Made of muslin stretched over a thin frame of wood and wire, the early planes were flimsy and precarious. The Wright brothers had only just completed their first successful flight in 1903. Some people thought that airplanes were still a joke, a silly idea that would never catch on.

"If God meant people to fly, they would have wings," some said. But Katherine was fascinated by these new machines, the money she might earn, and the chance to fly with the birds. Nothing could discourage her.

She got her first chance to ride in an airplane in January 1912.

"People had filled my ears with all sorts of stories of how I would feel—of the fright, the dizziness, the airsickness and all sorts of things," Katherine said. But none of them happened. Katherine's 20 minute flight excited her so much that she hated to land. She was now determined to become a pilot.

Who would teach Katherine to fly? There were fewer than 200 licensed pilots in the whole world at the time. Only three of them were women. But Katherine was determined to learn how to fly, and she sought out one of the most famous early aviators, Max Lillie of Chicago. She asked him to teach her.

He took one look at Katherine and said, "No!"

Katherine stood only a little over five feet tall and weighed only 101 pounds. She looked like she might be 12 years old, instead of 21, and Lillie just didn't think this "little girl" was strong enough to manage his two-handled "pusher" airplane.

Right. Mrs. Emma Stinson, center, encouraged both of her daughters to be courageous. Katherine, right, once said, "My mother never warned me not to do this or that for fear of being hurt. Of course I got hurt, but I was never afraid."

Below. Katherine inspired her younger brothers, Eddie and Jack, to follow flying careers. In 1914, Katherine gave Jack one of his first airplane rides.

Far right. Katherine flew this open-air plane at Fort Sam Houston in San Antonio around 1914.

Aultman Collection, El Paso Public Library

John Underwood, Glendale, CA

He patiently explained to her that the pilot had to handle two shoulder-high sticks to control the height and angle of the wings of the airplane. The propeller was at the rear of the plane, and the pilot's seat was on the front edge of the lower wing. The cockpit was like a giant swing with wings attached to each side, and the propeller in back pushed the pilot and the whole machine up into the air. Nothing separated the pilot from the vast sky. And the pilot had to guide the clumsy machine with those two big sticks. Max Lillie thought it was too much for most men to handle —but it would be impossible for this curly-haired girl!

He underestimated Katherine. She finally persuaded Lillie to take her up in one of his planes, and she proved to him that size, strength and sex had nothing to do with being a pilot. What was required was clear thinking, calmness, dexterity and determination. And Katherine had those qualities in abundance.

After only four hours of flight time with Max Lillie, Katherine flew alone. She loved it. And on July 12, 1912, she passed the test to earn her pilot's license. She became the fourth woman pilot in America.

Katherine tucked her long curls under a helmet, put on a coat and knee-high boots like the famous aviators wore and began to fly the air show circuit. She loved to take her machine into the sky, turn it sideways, fly it upside down and fling it into head-spinning circles.

And people loved to watch her. There was something exciting about watching this pretty young woman undertake daring stunts in those strange flying machines. Farm families and small-town residents who had only seen pictures of the new airplanes flocked to county fairs to see this "Flying Schoolgirl" soar above them among the puffy white clouds.

Katherine loved the sensation of flying.

"When you are flying toward a cloud it does not seem as if you, yourself, are moving. The cloud seems to be rushing at you. And when you enter it you are in the thickest fog you ever imagined. You can't see the wings of your plane. I have been in clouds so dense that I couldn't even see my own hands operating the controls."

Flying in the open-air cockpits didn't always create such pleasant sensations, however. Katherine compared flying in the rain without a windshield to being "peppered with buckshot. The raindrops sting your face like sleet driven by a gale."

Katherine flew her aircraft into a thunderstorm once.

"Lightning would streak right between the wings of my machine. It is a very curious thing to see it so close to you," she said.

Katherine wasn't frightened at the time, but when she learned that some airplanes had been struck by lightning while being flown in thunderstorms, she decided not to take any more chances. She tried to limit her flights to good weather.

Katherine flew in air shows at county and state fairs in Ohio, Georgia, Arkansas, Texas, Louisiana and hundreds of other places. She, and other stunt pilots, introduced flying to thousands of Americans. People began to believe there might be more to this new adventure than a few tricks and thrills in the air.

Katherine's family decided that her love for flying might provide a new business opportunity for them. In 1913, Katherine's mother, Emma Stinson, joined Katherine in founding the Stinson Aviation Company in Hot Springs, Arkansas, the family's current home. They began to build, sell and rent aircraft. Katherine's love of flying not only made her forget her dreams of a music career, but it also opened up a whole new way of life for her entire family. Katherine's younger sister, Marjorie, and her younger brothers, Jack and Eddie, also fell in love with flying. So did people all over the United States.

Katherine's instructor, Max Lillie, went to San Antonio, Texas, in 1912. The winters were mild there and pilots could fly almost every day without worrying about bad weather. Steady winds and flat terrain created ideal conditions for flying.

Lillie had persuaded the United States Army to let him use the parade grounds of Fort Sam Houston as a flying field. Military officers were interested in watching the progress of the new aviation business to see if airplanes might be useful in warfare.

Max Lillie encouraged Katherine to move to San Antonio in 1913 to continue her flying. She decided to give it a try. She, too, was delighted with the ideal flight conditions. And she persuaded her family to move there with her. They eventually leased city land to establish the Stinson School of Flying.

Katherine practiced her stunts over the military parade grounds, and her Wright Model-B plane became a familiar sight to the people of San Antonio. However, some of Katherine's stunts caused alarm.

The San Antonio Light newspaper noted that "Miss Katherine Stinson, the girl aviator who is making daily flights in her aeroplane at Fort Sam Houston, must not attempt to loop-the-loop in the air or execute other aeronautical stunts that are dangerous to her life."

Everyone considered the loop-the-loop stunt particularly dangerous. To perform the stunt, the pilot headed the plane almost straight up into the air. At the top of the loop, the plane and its pilot were upside down. Then the pilot headed toward the ground to complete the circle, or loop, in the air. The danger was that the small airplane engine frequently stalled at the high point of the loop. A stalled plane fell freely, without any power or control, until the pilot could restart the engine. If the pilot was knowledgeable and experienced, he or she could usually go high enough to gain time to restart a stalled engine. But some pilots failed, and crowds always feared the pilot would crash during a loop-the-loop stunt. When the pilot succeeded, the crowd went wild with cheering applause.

Katherine taught herself to loop-the-loop and became the first woman to complete the stunt. In only six months Katherine had looped 500 times without an accident.

Katherine was a daring pilot, but she was not foolish. Most of her stunts were carefully planned and precisely executed. She took particularly good care of her aircraft and was one of the first pilots on the air show circuit to clean her plane before each performance. Some of the male pilots teased her because she went over every inch of her plane, scrubbing and polishing the wires and cleaning the joints. Katherine wrote in *The American Magazine* in 1917:

The men thought I was a regular old maid about it. They said I would ruin the

14

cloth with my scrubbing, and that the oil didn't hurt the wires and joints, anyway. . . . But I wanted to see the conditions of things under all that dirt. And I really did find that a good many wires needed to be replaced. It's all right if your automobile goes wrong while you are driving it. You can get out in the road and tinker with it. But if your airplane breaks down, you can't sit on a convenient cloud and tinker with that!

Katherine was not only a good pilot, she was also a good mechanic. Like many of the early pilots, she had to understand engines and have some mechanical ability. She knew how to take apart her whole plane and put it back together. In fact, each time Katherine traveled by train to an air show she carried her plane on the train, disassembling it for the trip and reassembling it at her destination. She studied and learned the

Katherine Stinson flew several different airplanes. All were biplanes, with two parallel wings, like the ones shown here. The circular arrow shows the pattern of Katherine's famous loop-the-loop stunt.

principles of aerodynamics and understood that a pilot could be only as good as the aircraft.

"The important thing is to be as careful as you possibly can to have every part of your engine and of your plane in perfect condition," Katherine said. She believed that most accidents occurred because of some failure of the machine, not from the pilot's lack of ability. She made sure her planes were safe and in good working condition *before* she undertook her daring stunts.

When she knew that her plane was in good working order, she would try anything. She added a snap roll on the top of her loop. She performed night exhibition flghts and dazzled crowds when she used fireworks on the tips of her wings.

- At a Long Island, New York, aviation tournament, she whirred through the air in darkness, then lit up the sky with fireworks and turned two somersaults. The crowd applauded wildly. Then the sky was black again. Suddenly the plane reappeared, with the fireworks aglow. Katherine did two spiral twists before landing triumphantly.
- In Los Angeles, California, in 1915, Katherine spelled out "Cal" with fireworks, becoming the first pilot to do night skywriting.
- In London, Katherine startled the conservative English who looked up in the sky and saw her plane sailing around the Houses of Parliament and the dome of St. Paul's Cathedral.
- In Canada, many people saw an airplane for the first time when Katherine entertained military troops with simulated bombing demonstrations.
- In Saskatchewan, Canada, she thrilled crowds with her nose dive but some of the spectators worried that she had crashed because her dive was so steep.
- In 1916, when Katherine toured Japan and China, she was the first woman to fly in those nations. Nearly 25,000 people turned out to see her Tokyo performance in December 1916. She flew for 15 minutes and traced the letter *S* in the sky with fireworks. The crowd loved it and nearly mobbed her airplane when she landed. The people of Japan, especially the women, overwhelmed her with tributes, calling her the "Air Queen." Stinson fan clubs sprang up all over Japan. In China, she made 32 flights, including a private exhibition for the Chinese leaders.

Katherine became world famous. She was called the "world's greatest woman pilot." Whenever she flew, thousands of people went to see her. Newspapers and magazines carried articles about her. Spectators and fellow aviators alike respected her flying abilities.

When the United States entered World War I, Katherine wanted to help her country. The U.S. Army had recognized the potential of aircraft to change the course of warfare and had issued a call for volunteer pilots. Katherine volunteered. But because she was a woman, the Army turned her down.

That didn't stop Katherine from working in the war effort. The American Red Cross started raising funds to assist with relief efforts, and Katherine volunteered to help once again. This time her offer was accepted.

In the summer of 1917, Katherine flew from Buffalo, New York, to Washington, D.C., dropping Red Cross fundraising leaflets. She also collected pledges for money at stops along the way. She performed some razzle-dazzle, too.

On the way into Albany, she spotted the Empire State Express train speeding down the track to the same destination. Flying just 300 feet above the train and delighting its passengers, Katherine raced the train. She beat it into Albany by 34 minutes.

When she reached the nation's capital at the end of her fundraising tour, she circled the Washington Monument and then landed near a cheering throng of 5,000. At the Treasury Building, she presented the Secretary of the Treasury $2 million in Red Cross pledges.

Katherine was now 26 years old and had been flying for five years. Military flying was out, so she decided she would try for a major aviation record. Her friend and fellow aviator Ruth Law had set a long distance record of 512 miles in 1916, and Katherine was determined to better it.

Katherine ordered a special airplane, one with a maximum air speed of 85 miles per hour and the capability of traveling 700 miles before refueling. (Like her other airplanes, this one had a built-in mirror, so she could clean her face and dab on some makeup before meeting the press upon landing.)

Katherine decided to set her record by flying the San Diego to San Francisco route, over the

Katherine's fame spread worldwide when she toured the Orient in 1916.
Above. More than 25,000 Japanese welcomed her to Tokyo.
Right. Katherine also flew over these Chinese spectators in Peking.

treacherous mountains of Southern California.

At 7:31 a.m. on December 11, 1917, her small open-air plane sped off a dirt runway in San Diego into the foggy Southern California sky. Its destination, San Francisco, lay 610 miles away — farther than any pilot had ever flown without stopping.

Katherine completed the first leg to Los Angeles with relative ease. But past Los Angeles, she began to lift the plane higher and higher, over the jagged Tehachapi Mountains and through treacherous winds.

The cold head wind sliced into her plane, cut her lips and chilled her to the bone. She coaxed the plane to 9,000 feet, higher than she had ever flown before.

Time moved slowly. Katherine had forgotten to pack a lunch, and she was hungry. If she could just make it over the mountains, she would be fine. The Santa Fe Railroad tracks served as her guide through the mountains. Suddenly they disappeared. Was she lost? Had she let the plane drift off course? Would she ever find her way out of the mountains?

A less experienced pilot might have panicked, but Katherine remained calm and waited, staying firmly on course. Her patience was rewarded when the railroad tracks reappeared below her. They had been hidden from her view as they ran into a long mountain tunnel. Katherine breathed a sigh of relief as she pulled her plane out of the mountains.

19

"Beyond Tehachapi, the sky cleared. The beautiful California landscape spread under me like a huge painting as I sped along at the rate of 62 miles per hour," she recounted.

"I remember that at noon I looked down and saw people going home to dinner and I imagined I could smell the food cooking. I was faint with hunger by that time and the temptation to land and get something to eat was almost irresistible. But I stuck it out."

Katherine had other things on her mind besides food. She had to concentrate on conserving fuel and staying on course.

"Occasionally I shifted my map mounted on rollers, so I could handle a great length of it. It was easy to tell where I was all the time . . . towns, cities, farms, hills and mountains passed rapidly . . . I never had any fear. The main thing was speed."

She described her historic landing: "I circled around the Golden Gate and found the Presidio (an Army fort in San Francisco). Tears came to my eyes as I heard the cheers of thousands of soldiers down below. They were lined up in two files and I landed between them. They rushed up and helped me out of my plane and I was mighty proud."

On the San Francisco waterfront, ships and vessels of all types blew horns to give her a noisy welcome. It was 4:41 p.m. Katherine had flown 610 miles in nine hours and ten minutes. She had just two gallons of fuel left in her tank. She had flown longer and covered more miles than any aviator in the world, man or woman. Katherine had set a record; her place in the history of aviation was assured. When she proved that she was the world's greatest long-distance flyer that December day in 1917, she became an international star.

She was a heroine all right — but she would never be a war heroine. Despite her expertise and world acclaim, the government still refused to let her fly in the combat area. She again applied for a job as a World War I reconnaissance pilot, but was turned down once more.

Katherine Stinson kept an eye on the construction of airplanes she had specially designed for long-distance flights. She carefully inspected her planes before each flight and kept every part in working order.

20

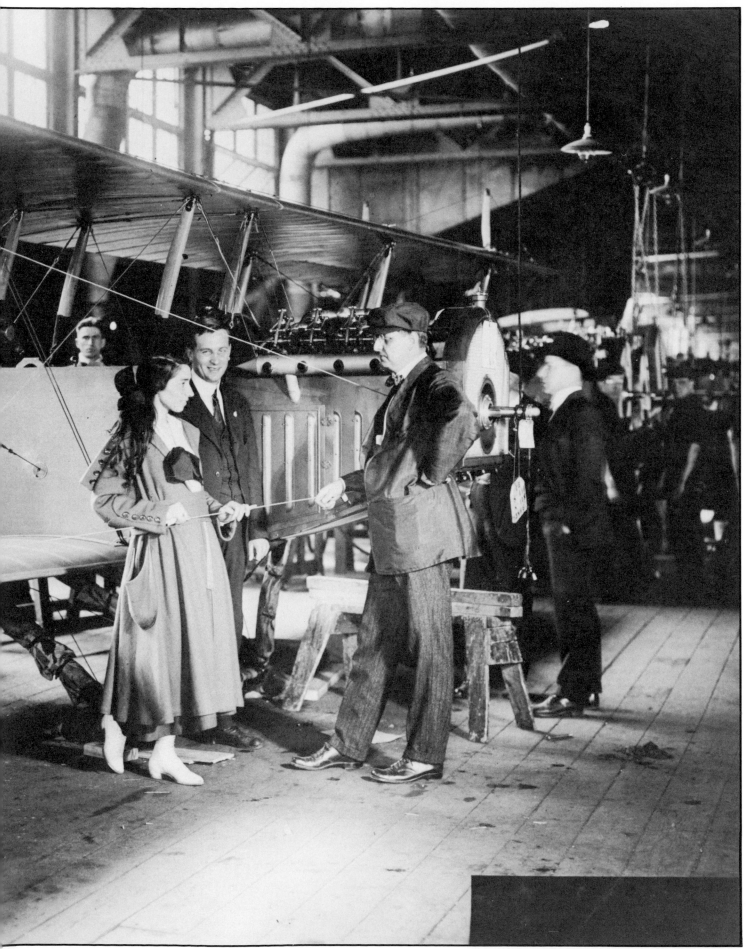

So Katherine had to be content with being the first woman to fly the mail in this country. And she set another aviation record doing so.

One day in May 1918, she set out to fly the mail nonstop from Chicago to New York, a record distance. But she ran into trouble. She hit heavy head winds and ran out of fuel 150 miles short of New York City. She landed on a hillside near Binghamton, New York, and her plane nosed over in the mud. But the shortened flight of 783 miles broke her own long-distance record. Later, she wrote about that flight, revealing a lot about her sheer determination.

"I had been sick in bed for five days before I made that flight . . . I was pretty weak and shaky and had a high temperature, but I had set my heart on making that flight. After all, you have to choose which is going to rule, your mind or your body . . . If you determine that it shall be your mind, your body will surprise you by the way it bucks up and behaves itself.

"At four-thirty in the morning I went to the hangar, gave the machine another minute examination and at six-thirty I was off. If the wind had been favorable, I should have made the flight to New York without stops. As it was, I broke both the distance and the endurance record in this country. That seems to me more worthwhile than staying in bed with nothing to show for it but doctors' bills."

As a mail carrier, she flew the New York to Washington route. But after only a short time with the air mail service, Katherine decided to quit.

The United States war effort still enticed her. She refused to wait any longer to help — even if she couldn't be a pilot. So Katherine, the expert pilot, became an expert ambulance driver in World War I. She served in London and France, driving wounded soldiers to safety. But the rough wartime conditions and harsh winter climate damaged her health, as her daring stunt flights had never done.

At the end of the war, Katherine contracted influenza, which was later diagnosed as tuberculosis. She fought a six-year battle to recover from the disease. The treatment was rest and withdrawal from her previously active life. She moved to Santa Fe, New Mexico. Her spectacular flying career ended.

In 1928, Katherine married Miguel Otero, Jr., a former World War I airman. Although Katherine never flew again, her inquiring mind and renewed energy led her to take up a new career. She studied architecture and became an award-winning home designer.

Katherine lived to be 86 years old. She never gave in to the fear that prevents people from trying to do something they believe is important.

"Fear as I understand it, is simply due to lack of confidence or lack of knowledge — which is the same thing," Katherine said. "You are afraid of what you don't understand, of the things you cannot account for. You are afraid to attempt something you believe you cannot do."

Katherine was not afraid. She believe in herself, her abilities and her dreams. She believed that "we can fly." And she did.

Marjorie Stinson taught military flying and gunnery techniques to World War I cadets at the Stinson School of Flying in San Antonio.

W.D. Smithers Collection, Humanities Research Center, The University of Texas at Austin

The Flying Schoolmarm
MARJORIE STINSON

(1896–1975)

She was known as the "flying schoolmarm." That's because Marjorie Stinson, Katherine's younger sister, established her reputation as a teacher — a flight instructor. Although Marjorie never achieved Katherine's fame, she was well-known in aviation circles and even flew the air show circuit for a while.

After earning her pilot's license in 1914 when she was only 18, Marjorie thrilled audiences across Texas and the nation with her stunt flying. One of her favorite stunts was to go high in the air, turn her plane sideways and drop straight down 1,500 feet. Then as the audience screamed, she suddenly righted the plane and sailed calmly over their heads.

In 1915, Marjorie began training pilots at the family-owned Stinson School of Flying in San Antonio. Most of her students were young Canadian men who were eager to fight with the Allies in World War I. Because her school was the only one in the U.S. that was open all winter, group after group of would-be pilots came to San Antonio to learn from Marjorie. She was considered to be one of the best flight instructors in the nation. In all, Marjorie trained more than 80 Canadian and American pilots for war duty.

Marjorie not only flew the air show circuit and trained pilots, she also flew Texas's first airmail flights, along the San Antonio to Seguin route.

And she worked in the U.S. War Department as an aeronautical draftswoman for 15 years. After her retirement, Marjorie devoted herself to researching the history of aviation. She died in 1975, two years before Katherine. Stinson Field in San Antonio, once the home of her flight school, is now part of the municipal airport system of the City of San Antonio.

24

Babe Didrikson Zaharias was a Norwegian immigrant's daughter from Beaumont, Texas, who became one of the most famous people in the world.

When she died, the President of the United States opened his press conference with a tribute to her.

Babe Didrikson Zaharias made her name in a way no woman had done before—through her sheer athletic ability. She won more medals and set more records in more sports than any other athlete, male or female, in the twentieth century.

She won three Olympic medals for track and field. She was an All-America basketball player. She won every major women's golf championship in the world.

Mildred "Babe" Didrikson Zaharias first became a hero when the American public was starved for heroes in the Depression year of 1932. She stunned the sports world by winning a national championship track meet all by herself. Her one-person team beat out the second place team 30 points to 22. And the second place team had 22 members!

Two weeks later, she won two gold medals and a silver medal at the international Olympic games. The country went wild. She was called "Wonder Girl," "The Texas Tornado," "The Terrific Tomboy."

Women athletes have come into their own since Babe Didrikson Zaharias's early exploits. Although girls' basketball programs had been popular in Texas public schools since the turn of the century, only a few other athletic events were open to women. Some schools had sports programs for women, but most did not. Beginning in 1972, federal laws (Title IX of the Education Act) required public schools and colleges to spend as much money on sports programs for girls as for boys. Now girls have many of the same opportunities that boys do to excel at basketball, track, swimming, soccer, tennis, golf and most other sports.

Babe Didrikson Zaharias would have been an outstanding athlete at any time in history. But her unusual talent, courage and determination made her the greatest athlete of the twentieth century. This is her story.

The World's Greatest Athlete
BABE DIDRIKSON ZAHARIAS

(1912–1956)

Babe was everything a girl wasn't supposed to be.

She was boastful, competitive, brash—and athletic.

Girls her age in the 1920s and early 1930s were supposed to be sweet and passive. Most were happy sideline supporters of the boys' sports activities. Babe, however, refused to sit on the sidelines. She wanted to compete.

She cared nothing about playing with dolls, dressing pretty or going to dances. She picked fights, played practical jokes and dared her schoolmates to compete with her.

In high school, a big football player once stepped up to her, stuck out his chin, and said he doubted she could hurt him no matter what she tried. She swung once, hit him, and he dropped to the floor senseless.

Although she was born in Port Arthur, Babe grew up in a working-class neighborhood of Beaumont. She played with the rough neighborhood boys and got used to being "smashed around" in games, as she later put it.

She was the only girl in the neighborhood sandlot baseball games. She hit so many home runs that the kids began to call her "Babe" after the national baseball hero of the time, Babe Ruth.

Babe's father was a carpenter from Norway. Her parents were poor, often struggling to raise a family of seven children. They lived in a small two-bedroom house.

The Didriksons were an athletic family. Babe's mother, Hannah, had been an excellent ice skater in Norway. Babe's older brothers competed in football, baseball and boxing. Competition was in Babe's blood.

Babe's parents couldn't afford expensive athletic equipment for their children. Instead, Babe trained on makeshift gymnastic equipment her father built in their backyard. She swung from a trapeze, jumped over bars and lifted weights.

She even set up her own "hurdling" course over seven hedges on the block between her house and the corner grocery.

Always looking for adventure and challenge, Babe mastered the trapeze and the tightrope with hopes of joining a circus someday.

Then in 1928, Babe heard about the Olympics and decided she wanted to compete. When she learned she would have to wait four years until the next Olympic Games in 1932, Babe was disappointed. But she decided she would compete then, no matter what. So she began to prepare herself for the greatest athletic contest in the world.

Babe became her high school's star basketball player. At first, the coach of the girls' team said that she was too short. But she stayed after school and practiced with the boys until the girls' team let her try out. After making the team, she was high scorer from the start.

Babe's school had a sports program for girls, and she played on every girls' team available — volleyball, tennis, golf, baseball, basketball, swimming. In fact, she tried to join the boys' football team as a place kicker, but the coach refused.

Babe's formal entry into the sports world came in 1930, when a Dallas company recruited her to play on its basketball team. In those days, big companies often sponsored teams for their employees. The firm, Employers Casualty Insurance, wanted Babe to quit school, come to work for them and play on their team. She and her family decided that Babe could leave school for a few months, then return to Beaumont to finish her last year.

Babe, 18 years old, had never been more than a few miles from her home. The trip to Dallas, 275 miles away from Beaumont, was "like going to Europe," she said.

Babe arrived in Dallas February 17, 1930, and played her first game February 18. She soon became the best player in the league. She once scored 106 points in a single game. And when playing the defending champion team from Sun Oil, Babe scored more points then the entire Sun Oil team combined.

She led the Golden Cyclones of Employers Casualty to the national championship. Babe was named All-America player in 1930, 1931 and 1932.

Babe's boss, Colonel M. J. McCombs, decided to organize a track and field team to give Babe a chance to excel in that sport.

When the team was formed, Babe asked McCombs, "Colonel, how many events are there in this track and field?"

"Why Babe," he answered, "I think there are about nine or ten."

"Well, I'm going to do them all," Babe told him.

And she did. In her first meet, she entered ten events and won eight of them. She achieved her best marks in the high jump, and in running hurdles and throwing the javelin.

While she worked for Employers Casualty and played on their team, Babe broke three national track and field records and helped win 17 loving cups and 92 medals. She held the Southern Amateur Athletic Union (AAU) record in every track and field event she entered from 1930 to 1932.

Then came her big opportunity. In 1932, the AAU national championship track meet in Chicago also served as the Olympic trials. If Babe won this meet, she could go on to compete in the Olympic games later that year.

Colonel McCombs had such confidence in Babe's abilities that she was the only athlete he sent to Chicago. She was the only one-person "team" in the stadium on opening day.

"I spurted out there all alone, waving my arms, and you never heard such a roar. It brought goose bumps all over me," she said.

Babe's heart pounded as she went through her warm-up exercises before the first event. Her muscular body, now grown lanky and lean, was tense with excitement. She couldn't let those cheering people down, no matter what! But as she settled into position for the first race, Babe knew that the only thing she must think about was the race itself. Nothing else must break her concentration — not the cheers of the crowd, not even her dreams for the Olympics. Winning this particular race was the most important thing in her life.

At the instant the shot from the starting gun rang out, Babe thrust her body forward. Her strong legs pushed her faster than she had ever run before — faster than she believed possible. She surged past the other runners, one by one. She was almost there. One last burst of energy propelled her through the tape at the finish line.

Babe was gasping for breath as she continued on down the track. Then she realized that the steady roar of the crowd had turned into cheering, shouting approval. She really *had* won! It was exhilarating! If this is what it meant to be a champion, then Babe wanted more.

She got her wish that day in Chicago. Of the eight events she entered, she won first place in five of them. And she beat her own world records in the javelin throw and in the 80-meter hurdles. A reporter covering the track meet called it, "the most amazing series of performances ever accomplished by any individual, male or female, in track and field history." And, of course, Babe qualified for the Olympics.

It was the beginning of the Babe Didrikson legend.

Newspapers splashed her name across sports pages throughout the country. She was no longer just a young girl from Texas who played sports well. She was a national phenomenon.

The Chicago track meet confirmed Babe's growing belief in her own abilities. Ever since she was a little girl, Babe had felt that she was special. She always knew that she had extraordinary strength, speed and endurance. And now, with one public triumph after another, Babe was beginning to develop the determination and self-discipline that only the most exceptional people in the world possessed. Babe knew that as long as she had the "will to win," her natural athletic talents would make winning possible.

She had so much confidence in herself now that it just spilled over in her conversations with friends, and even with members of the press. And they loved her for it. How refreshing it was for them to find that this pleasant young woman told the truth about her feelings and her desire to win.

The great Babe Didrikson Zaharias excelled at more sports than any man or woman during the first half of the 20th century. During her 25 years of competition, she astounded the world with an extraordinary athletic ability.

As she began to prepare for the Olympic games in Los Angeles, the newspaper writers quoted her again and again.

"I came out to beat everybody in sight and that's just what I'm going to do," she said. "Sure, I can do anything."

She told the press: "Yep, I'm going to win the high jump Sunday and set a world record. I don't know who my opponents are and, anyways, it wouldn't make any difference."

Talking in her Texas twang, she became a legendary character, a country charmer. She was refreshing to the millions of newspaper readers who were suffering from hard economic times during the Great Depression. She inspired Americans because she believed she would win. Her self-confidence lifted their own.

"All I know is that I can run and I can jump and I can toss things and when they fire a gun or tell me to get busy I just say to myself, 'Well, kid, here's where you've got to win another.' And I usually do."

Still, she didn't neglect her serious training. Babe even exercised and jogged in the aisles on the train going out to Los Angeles.

Out of five Olympic women's events, a competitor could enter a maximum of three. So Babe entered three.

She won the javelin throw with a new world's record, breaking the old record by an astounding 11 feet.

She broke her own world record in the 80-meter hurdles with a time of 11.7 seconds. She tied for first place in the high jump, but was awarded second place when the officials ruled she had dived forward, rather than jumped.

The result: two gold medals and one silver.

Again, Babe was the darling of the sportswriters. One writer called her, "without any question, the athletic phenomenon of all time, man or woman."

The day after her Olympic triumph, sportswriter Grantland Rice invited her to play a round of golf with several other male sportswriters. Babe had played golf before, in high school and in Dallas. But she had never taken serious lessons or practiced it on a regular basis.

That day in Los Angeles, she rared back, swung hard, and hit the ball farther than any of the men. She turned in a respectable score of 95.

Babe, center, stands proudly on the winner's platform at the 1932 Olympics where she won one silver and two gold medals. Babe set a new world record in the 80-meter hurdles.

Above. **The city of Dallas threw a gala parade and ''welcome home'' celebration when Babe returned triumphant from the 1932 Olympics.**

Right. **After the Olympics, Babe took up golf and won all the major women's championships. Her successes enabled her to vastly increase opportunities for women in professional golf.**

The sportswriters, who were some of her biggest fans, declared her a potential golf champion.

But Babe didn't take up golf right away.

After all the glamour and hoopla of the Olympics had died down, Babe had to decide how she was going to make a living.

Over the years, Babe had tried nearly every sport and mastered all of them. She could swim. She played a mean game of billiards. She was an excellent tennis player. She always scored over 200 in bowling. In Dallas, she gave fancy diving exhibitions. She once socked in 13 home runs in a double-header softball game.

Had she been a man, she might have earned a living by playing on a professional basketball or baseball team. But few professional sports were open for women. And so Babe briefly tried show business. She performed on stage in red, white and blue jacket and satin shorts; she made some movies and went on a promotional basketball tour; she even toured as a pitcher with a men's promotional baseball team.

But her new career, she finally decided, would be golf.

Babe spent the summer of 1933 taking golf lessons. She described her first day as a golf student:

"I had my shower and breakfast and was ready to leave for the driving range by five o'clock in the morning. It wasn't daylight yet, but rather than just sit around, I went out there.

"I had a golf club and I practiced what he'd (the teacher) told me about the stance. Finally they came and opened up the place, and Stan and I hit balls all day long."

By this time, Babe had spent almost all the money she had earned on her various promotional tours as an Olympic star. Her former employer, Employers Casualty, came to her rescue and offered Babe another job. The firm obtained a membership for her at the Dallas Country Club and paid for her golf lessons. Steadily she improved her stroke and her strategy.

In November 1934, Babe entered her first golf tournament. When asked what score she thought she'd make in the first round, she replied, half-joking, "I think I'll shoot a 77" (an excellent golf score). Sure enough, the next day, the headlines declared, "Wonder Girl Makes Her Debut in Tournament Golf: Turns in 77 Score."

In golf, as in every other sport that Babe tried, she had enormous natural ability. But she still believed in practice.

She practiced 12 to 16 hours at a stretch on the golf course on weekends. During the work week, Babe got up at 5:30 a.m. and practiced until it was time to go to work at the insurance office. At noon, she quickly ate a sandwich and devoted the remainder of her lunch hour to golf—practicing putting on the carpet of her boss's office.

And then she'd practice some more. Sometimes, "I'd hit balls until my hands were bloody and sore," she recalled. "I'd have tape all over my hands and blood all over the tape."

Her work paid off in 1935. Babe won her first major tournament, the Texas State Women's Golf Championship.

Babe's competitive golf efforts, however, were clouded by concern about whether she was considered an "amateur" or a "professional" player.

In the sports world, amateurs received no prize money or salaries for their efforts. Professionals, on the other hand, competed for prizes or money. Some were even paid salaries. Professionals and amateurs rarely competed against each other; their athletic contests were kept separated.

Babe had entered and won the Texas State Women's Golf Championship as an amateur. Even though she won, she received no prize money. However, Babe had been paid when she played basketball and baseball before.

Was Babe a professional or an amateur?

The United States Golf Association said that since Babe had been paid for *some* sports, she was a professional in *all* sports. As a result, the Association declared Babe ineligible to play amateur women's golf. This move cut Babe off from competitive women's golf because there were no professional women's tournaments. Babe was crushed.

Babe loved golf too much to give it up. So she decided to demonstrate her golf talents in "celebrity" golf matches with some of the best male golfers and entertainers in the United States. She delighted crowds all over the country when she often hit the ball farther than the men.

After playing with Babe, comedian Bob Hope once told reporters, "There's only one thing wrong with Babe and myself. I hit the ball like a girl and she hits it like a man."

Babe's "celebrity" matches took her to the richest country clubs in the nation. She played with boxing champion Joe Louis and baseball superstar Ted Williams. She even got to play with the great baseball legend Babe Ruth. Later, she became friends with a world-famous golfer who lived in the White House, President Dwight D. Eisenhower.

During one of Babe's golf tours, she met George Zaharias, a professional wrestler. They married in December 1938, and George began to devote his life to managing Babe's career.

Because Babe missed playing competitively, she and George continued to try to persuade the U.S. Golf Association to reinstate her as an amateur so that she could enter tournaments. They succeeded in 1943 when the U.S. Association reversed its earlier ruling. Babe was able to play tournament golf again as an amateur.

Babe tore up the courses in the 1940s, and was named Outstanding Woman Athlete of the Year in 1945. She won the National Women's Amateur Tournament in 1946, the beginning of an amazing winning streak of 17 tournaments. (The longest streak in men's golf had been 11 tournament victories.)

Babe was winning every golf tournament in sight—even the British Women's Amateur Championship in 1947. But she was running out of challenges and longed for even greater competition.

In 1948, Babe once again turned professional. She even tried to enter the men's national open tournament. When she was refused entry, she and her husband organized the Ladies Professional Golf Association (LPGA). It was the beginning of a dramatic rise in the prestige and recognition of women's professional golf. Total prize money rose from $15,000 in 1949 to nearly $250,000 in 1955.

Babe Didrikson Zaharias was winning a lot of that money. She won the Western Open, the U.S. Women's Open, the All-American and World championships—every title there was to win. In her golf career, Babe won an amazing 82 tournaments. In 1949, the Associated Press named Babe the Outstanding Female Athlete of the Half-Century.

Mazzulla Collection, Amon Carter Museum, Fort Worth

Above. Once Babe became a celebrity, she played exhibition golf with Hollywood stars. Here, she joined singer Bing Crosby, left, and comedian Bob Hope, right.

Right. She also played golf with her friend who lived in the White House—President Dwight D. Eisenhower.

A big part of Babe's popularity was her folksy humor and her informal, personal style. Once a woman asked her for the secret to the way she hit a golf ball.

Babe replied, "It's not just enough to swing at the ball. You've got to loosen your girdle and really let the ball have it."

In April 1953, Babe played in the "Babe Zaharias Open," created in her honor in Beaumont. Though she had not been feeling well, she was determined to compete in this event. She managed to win, but did not feel the exhilaration that usually accompanied a victory.

The next morning she visited her family doctor. His diagnosis was intestinal cancer. Babe faced major surgery. At the hospital, Babe received 20,000 letters of encouragement.

Babe took her golf clubs with her to the hospital as a symbol of her determination to play competitive golf again. Sure enough, just three and a half months after her cancer surgery, Babe played in a tournament. She didn't win, but she captured the admiration of everyone, especially those who were fighting cancer themselves.

U.S. Postal Service

Above. The United States Post Office issued a special stamp in Babe's honor in 1981.
Right. Babe took her golf clubs to the hospital with her when she was treated for cancer in the 1950s. Although she ultimately lost her life to the disease in 1956, Babe's courage inspired millions of Americans.

No one thought Babe would ever win again. But in 1954, Babe won the National Women's Open and three other major tournaments. Even though she was not winning as consistently as before, Babe refused to retire. She wanted to continue her work promoting women's professional golf and inspiring other cancer patients.

But in June 1955, doctors found another trace of cancer and hospitalized her again. This time it was hopeless.

On the morning of September 26, 1956, President Dwight Eisenhower opened his White House press conference by saying, "Ladies and gentlemen, I should like to take one minute to pay tribute to Mrs. Zaharias, Babe Didrikson. She was a woman who in her athletic career certainly won the admiration of every person in the United States, all sports people over the world. I think every one of us feels sad that finally she had to lose this last one of all battles."

Babe Didrikson Zaharias was dead at age 45.

As a child, she had jumped over hurdles in her Beaumont neighborhood, nurturing a dream of the Olympics. She made the Olympics and more.

She caught the imagination of the American public as an athletic superstar who still maintained her down-home manner.

Babe did all this against great odds. All her life, from childhood on, she had to go against all of society's ideas about what a girl should do.

At times, she was ridiculed, even called a freak.

Instead of knuckling under, Babe held her head high and countered with her brash confidence and country girl charm.

She knew she had incredible physical ability, and she didn't let anyone stop her from taking that talent as far as it would go.

It took her to the top. She is remembered today as probably the most versatile athlete of the twentieth century. She is honored in at least ten halls of fame. There is a Babe Didrikson Zaharias Museum in Beaumont filled with her medals and trophies. In 1981, a commemorative U.S. postage stamp was issued featuring a photo of Babe caught in the exhilaration of another victory.

In a world where achievement can be measured by points, speed, distance and final scores, Babe was simply and undeniably the best there was.

38

When Dr. Sofie Herzog came to Texas in the 1890s, there were few doctors in the state—men or women. Texas didn't get its first medical school until 1891, and the few physicians who practiced in Texas had been educated elsewhere. Most medical schools in the eastern United States refused to allow women to study and learn to become physicians. Prejudice kept women out of the medical profession —some considered women too "delicate" to withstand the rigors of examining bodies and dealing with serious illness and death.

But women have always been society's healers. They assisted each other at childbirth and administered medicines or remedies long before the practice of medicine became a profession, with its requirements for specialized schooling and licensing. Women in the West were particularly active in the healing traditions. Because there were so few physicians on the frontier, women cared for children, created home remedies, nursed neighbors, and sat with dying friends and relatives.

Texas, like most other western states, never legally prohibited women from attending medical school. But many officials discouraged them from doing so. It was 1897 before the first two women graduated from medical schools in Texas. Not even nursing was taken seriously as a profession for women until 1909, when the Texas Legislature passed standards and procedures for licensing nurses.

Dr. Sofie Herzog was somewhat of an oddity, then, when she arrived in Brazoria, Texas, around 1893. But she didn't let prejudice, ridicule or gossip stop her from doing what she believed she must do—provide the best medical service possible. Dr. Sofie Herzog worked hard to build a life for herself in the rough atmosphere of the southeast coast of Texas. She believed in her profession, and she believed in herself. This is her story.

The Daring Doctor of Brazoria
DR. SOFIE HERZOG

(1848–1925)

She was a daring doctor in a gunfighter's town. She galloped across rustic Texas trails and hopped railroad cars to reach her patients. She treated bandits for gunshot wounds and made a necklace out of the bullets she removed from them.

She was Sofie Herzog, the mother of 14 children who became the unlikely town doctor in the coastal community of Brazoria, Texas in the 1890s. She was one of only a handful of Texas's women doctors at the time. But few of them were as daring as "Dr. Sofie."

She shocked townspeople by wearing short hair and a man's hat. She rode astride her horse, instead of sidesaddle the way most ladies did. But over a 30-year career, she endeared herself to the people of Brazoria who came to admire her medical skill and her tender devotion to the sick and wounded.

Sofie was born in Austria in 1848, the daughter of an internationally known surgeon. At 14, she married a young surgeon and during their 26-year marriage, the couple had 14 children, including two sets of twins. The Herzogs lived in Vienna, the medical center of the world in the 19th century.

Around 1870, Sofie decided to study medicine so that she could assist her surgeon husband. She attended a Viennese university and observed world-famous surgeons at work. At home, she discussed the latest techniques and medical theories with her husband.

In 1886, her husband accepted a job in New York. The Herzogs said good-bye to their native land and started a new life in America. Sofie's husband had high hopes for a brilliant career in the United States, but only a few years after they arrived, Dr. Herzog died.

Sofie was just past 40 years old, alone in a strange country with children to support. What could she do? The only profession she knew was medicine. But in America, there was great prejudice and suspicion against women doctors.

Medicine was considered an "unladylike" occupation. A woman doctor had to examine unclothed bodies, and many people considered this almost scandalous. It was the height of the Victorian age when only the very poorest women worked, and middle-class women were considered too virtuous and fragile to be exposed to the hardship and dangers of the outside world. Most professions and careers were closed to women.

Sofie thought that was nonsense—as did a growing number of intelligent women. So Sofie decided to do what *she* thought was right and proper, no matter what anyone else said. After all, she was a trained physician. So she set up her medical practice in New York. She soon earned an excellent reputation and had many patients.

One day, Sofie's youngest daughter announced that she was getting married and going to Texas with her new husband.

Texas! Everyone knew it was a land of adventure. It had an untamed wilderness, filled with opportunities for enterprising individuals. Sofie

decided she wanted to go to Texas, too. After all, her children were beginning to build their own lives now. They really didn't need her supervision anymore.

Sofie was 45 years old and ready for a new adventure. She packed her medical instruments and supplies and headed for Texas! Sofie knew a life in Texas would be extremely different from sophisticated Vienna or progressive New York. Compared to those cities, life in Brazoria, Texas, would be primitive. But that didn't bother her. Sofie was ready for a change and a challenge.

People in Brazoria were very curious about their new woman doctor. As the sedate ladies of Brazoria peered out of their lace-curtained windows to look at the newly arrived Dr. Herzog, they shook their heads and muttered their disapproval. They saw an attractive woman with lively dark eyes. But she had *short* curly hair. The women were shocked. No woman in Brazoria had short hair! They all wore their long hair pinned up discretely on top of their heads — the way they thought all ladies should.

Undaunted by gossip and wagging tongues, Sofie went about the business of setting up a medical practice.

If Sofie wanted adventure, challenges and a new type of medical practice, she found it in

Brazoria. Most of her cases in those early years were gunshot victims. Bandits plagued the citizens of Brazoria County, and political battles were often fought with six-shooters.

Sofie became an expert at dislodging bullets. Her skill as a surgeon soon became well-known. She treated outlaws, saloon brawlers and feuding settlers. The lively town excited Sofie. It needed her skills. It began to value her services. Sofie had found a home.

Brazoria County, at the mouth of the Brazos River near the Gulf of Mexico, was still a primitive area with few roads. After a rain, its trails became muddy and passable only on horseback. Some of Sofie's patients lived along swampy river bottoms, among snakes and other wild animals. It was difficult to maneuver her wagon, and Sofie wanted to be able to get to her patients when they needed her. So she bought a beautiful horse for reliable transportation. She ordered a seamstress to make her a divided skirt.

Wearing a man's hat and her divided skirt, Sofie rode through the town astride her horse. The ladies were shocked once again. No "respectable" woman rode a horse like that! The proper way was sidesaddle — modestly and slowly. But Sofie wanted to get where she was going fast, and she galloped past the women on their porches, leaving them speechless. Sofie had no time for false modesty when patients needed her.

Sofie, like most small town doctors, practiced all kinds of medicine. She delivered babies, performed amputations and treated a variety of illnesses. She liked to mix her own medications for her patients, and she experimented with new methods of treatment.

Her daughter and son-in-law worried about her living alone and advised her to keep a gun handy. Sofie laughed and said she thought she could protect herself without a gun. She was right. One night a caller became troublesome and Sofie ordered him to leave. When he refused, she snatched up a poker from the fireplace and chased him out of her house. From then on, she proclaimed that the only weapon she needed was her trusty poker.

In 1905, the St. Louis, Brownsville and Mexico Railroad Company began laying track in Brazoria County. The influx of construction workers increased Sophie's business. Time and again they

were hurt in the serious accidents that happen when a railroad is built in an untamed land.

Many of these accident calls came to Sofie, who jumped on her horse and followed the faint trails into the woods to the construction site. Soon, the workers sang her praises and had complete confidence in this brave woman doctor.

In 1907, Sofie applied for the job of chief surgeon to the railroad. Railroad workers and local officials gave Dr. Herzog glowing recommendations and she was hired immediately.

But there was one problem. No one had told the railroad executives that Dr. Herzog was a woman! When the officials back East found this out, they withdrew their job offer. Being a railroad doctor was no job for a woman, they believed. It was rugged work, with long hours and many emergencies. They sent Sofie a letter, explaining their misunderstanding and saying they were confident she would resign.

Of course, Sofie did no such thing.

"I'll keep this job so long as I give satisfaction," she wrote back. "If I fail, then you can fire me."

Sofie never gave them a reason to fire her. She rode the train back and forth from Brazoria to Brownsville, treating sick and injured people along the way. Sometimes she rode in box cars, on hand cars, on engines — on anything that would get her quickly to the scene of the emergency.

Townspeople got used to the sight of "Dr. Sofie" whizzing by on a handcar with a railroad employee pumping frantically at top speed. People said, "Sofie clutched her hat with one hand and her doctor's bag with the other."

Over the years, many stories circulated about Sofie and her colorful personality. Visitors to her office came away with tales of her unusual animal collections. Some patients were shocked the first time they entered her office. Every inch of wall and floor space was covered with deer heads, stuffed birds and reptiles. All types of animal skins hung from the walls or served as rugs.

Sofie particularly liked snake skins. Men brought snakes to her office, and she hung them on the side of the buggy house to dry. Then she skinned them and mounted the skins on wide red satin ribbons. She collected the snake rattles too.

One day, Sofie decided she needed an alligator skin to add to her collection. A friend captured a seven-foot alligator and brought it to her office. He left it on the floor. Later that night, Sofie was preparing for bed when she heard a great crash

in her office. She dashed to the door and found the alligator moving. It was still very much alive.

Sofie grabbed her trusty poker and opened the front door. Then she stood on her bed and kept a nervous watch all night. Finally, the poor alligator lumbered slowly out of the office.

Sofie had another collection—one she wore around her neck. She saved all the bullets she extracted from gunshot victims and got a jeweler to string them between gold links. Twenty-four slugs eventually made up the unique necklace, and Sofie wore it constantly for good luck. She even requested that she be buried with it.

Eventually, Sofie became a leader in the community of Brazoria. She built and furnished a new Episcopal Church. Later she financed the construction of a two-story hotel across the street from her office.

When the first chugging automobiles appeared on the streets of Brazoria, Sofie just had to have one. By now, Sofie was an elderly woman, and people must have thought she was crazy to take a chance on driving the noisy, snorting early model cars. Sofie once again did as she pleased. She took a few driving lessons from the salesman

This is the kind of medical kit Sofie and other early doctors used. Her instruments included a saw for amputations, small knives for surgery and pliers for pulling teeth.

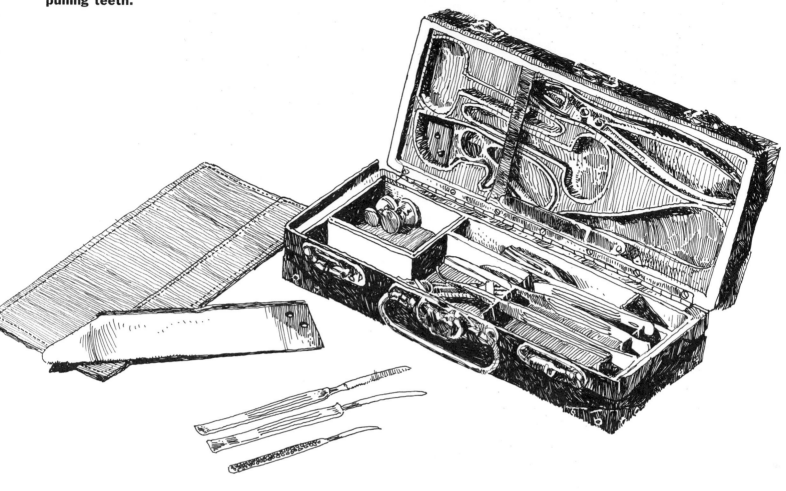

and then began making her rounds in her Ford "runabout."

When she was 65, Sofie married again. Her husband was Marion Huntington, the 70-year-old owner of a plantation between Freeport and Brazoria. She moved into his home and commuted seven miles over rough roads to her office every day for 11 years.

Sofie practiced medicine until 1925 — the year of her death. She was 76 years old. She had given 30 years of her life to the people of Brazoria County and the railroad workers up and down the Gulf Coast. She had used her medical talents in a place that badly needed competent doctors.

Many of Sofie's descendants stayed in Brazoria, including a granddaughter named after her.

Another grandchild, Alfred Herzog, became a surgeon, carrying on the tradition that dated back to his great-grandfather.

When she died, Sofie was honored for being one of the few women ever to serve as a railroad company surgeon. Her "professional skill and tenderness endeared her to all the Gulf Coast (work) force. The good she did lives after her," a newspaper article reported.

She was a woman who handled a rough job in a rugged place and did it exceptionally well. Like all women struggling to break into the professions at the time, she had to overcome ridicule and social disdain. But her abilities and courage eventually earned her the grateful respect of the community.

48

A lot of girls and boys dream about becoming famous movie or television stars, or of performing in front of an audience on the stage of a Broadway play. Margo Jones had a slightly different dream. Sure, she wanted the glamour, fame and excitement of stardom. But she wanted to direct the stars. She wanted to be behind the scenes, telling everyone else what to do and making sure that the audience enjoyed and understood the plays on the stage. Margo wanted to become a good enough stage director so that she could make other people famous stars.

Margo's hard work, talent and determination made her dream come true. She became one of the finest stage directors in the history of the American theater. Broadway producers wanted her to direct their plays. Actors and actresses wanted to work with her and learn from her.

Audiences enthusiastically flocked to her productions. Although she made her reputation in New York on the Broadway stage, it was in Texas in the late 1940s and 1950s that Margo did her finest work.

Margo believed that the only way to help young actors and actresses, and bright new playwrights, was to develop theaters away from Broadway and the expensive theater center in New York City. She envisioned small, regional theaters in all parts of the country, where a director could take a chance on producing a play by an exciting but unknown writer. Margo wanted to provide opportunities for talented young people to become stars. She wanted to try new stage techniques, experiment with lighting and sound, and bring plays to people who might otherwise never see them.

She got a chance to act on her beliefs when she set up a theater-in-the-round in Dallas, Texas, in 1947. It was a professional theater, with paid actors and actresses. It turned into one of the liveliest places on the American theater scene. Margo directed 85 plays there. Many of them were written by unknown playwrights who later became famous. Eight of them went on to become major Broadway hit plays.

Margo's Dallas theater changed the whole pattern of drama productions in America. After her success, regional theaters opened in Washington D.C., Los Angeles, San Francisco and other cities. Today, Southern Methodist University in Dallas operates the Margo Jones Experimental Theatre for its professional theater training program.

Margo Jones was truly a pioneer in the field of experimental American drama. This is her story.

The Director
MARGO JONES
(1912–1955)

When she was a little girl in Livingston, Texas, in the 1920s, Margaret Virginia Jones—nicknamed Margo—liked to dress in grownup costumes and pretend to be in a world of wonderous make-believe. And she liked to include other people in her make-believe world too.

By the time she was 11, Margo had coaxed her brothers and sisters into joining her in putting on plays for her family and neighbors in the barn. Margo hung up sheets to use as a stage curtain, dragged out her mother's and father's fancy old clothes and organized funny skits for entertainment on the long summer evenings.

Margo didn't act in those plays with the other kids. She *directed* them. She told everyone else how to act. She ran the rehearsals and helped the kids learn their lines. She created the sets and sold the tickets. Margo supervised the entire production!

All this time, Margo thought she wanted to become a lawyer, just like her father. She often followed her dad to the courtroom when he had to present a case. She loved to hear him make his impassioned speeches to the judge and jury. She loved the suspense while the jury deliberated about its verdict. Margo thought that nothing in the world was more entertaining than being in the courtroom with her father.

Then one day, it hit her! She realized that it was the *drama* of the courtroom that excited her — not the practice of law itself. Every courtroom trial told a story, just like the script of a play did. The lawyers and witnesses were like actors and actresses delivering their lines. The jury was the audience which had to decide who to believe and what decision to make. Organizing all of the action to make the presentation in the courtroom was a whole lot like organizing a play to put on for the neighbors! Margo was amazed. She didn't want to be a lawyer. She wanted to be a stage director!

By the time Margo was 14 years old, she took the first steps to become a director. She saw her first professional play in Fort Worth, a production of *Cyrano de Bergerac.* And she entered Texas State College for Women (now Texas Women's University) to major in drama. But all of the girls in her class wanted to be actresses. No one wanted to be a director, and Margo was too embarrassed to tell anyone what she wanted to do. In the theater most directors were men. Most women were actresses or costume designers.

What could Margo do? Should she dare to be different? Should she do something in the theater that most women didn't do? Wouldn't it be easier simply to give up her dream?

No, Margo decided. She would hold on to her dream. And she tried to learn everything she could about stage productions.

When a teacher suggested she read plays to learn what made a good script, Margo decided to read at least one play every day. And she did, for the rest of her life. From her reading, she learned exactly how good plays were structured. She learned how to build suspense — by keeping the audience from learning everything about the characters until the end of the play. She learned that when actors spoke lines which revealed strong emotions — fear, anger, sadness or joy — audiences got more involved in the play's action. And when audiences were emotionally involved, they enjoyed the play more. Margo learned that lighting, costumes and sets could help the audience suspend disbelief and imagine themselves involved in the action of the play.

51

Margo read, watched, learned and practiced her art. She even studied psychology so that she could better understand human motivation—the drama of everyday life.

During her last year in college, Margo went to a lecture by a famous drama critic. His job was to write about stage plays, to review them, for a newspaper audience, and he was on campus to speak to a group of journalism students. Margo sneaked in to hear him.

After his talk, to Margo's great surprise, he started a conversation with her.

"And what are you interested in?" he asked.

"I'm not supposed to be here," Margo replied nervously. "I'm in drama. I want to be a director."

Instead of laughing at her as she expected him to do, the drama critic told her he thought it was a great idea. He even offered to send her a booklet about directing.

This encouragement was all Margo needed. The day she received her college degree, she knocked on the door of the Southwestern School of Theater in Dallas and asked for a job. She was 19 years old. It was 1932, the middle of the Great Depression. Thousands of people were out of work and jobs were scarce.

"Can you type?" the interviewer asked her.

"Yes," answered Margo, who had typed her father's law briefs. Typing wasn't exactly what she had in mind, but at least it got her her first job in the theater.

Typically, Margo made the most of it. She observed the director of the school at work and studied his techniques to learn as much as she could about acting and directing.

In the summer of 1933, she enrolled at the Pasadena Summer School of Theater in California. There, she got what she needed most: respect and encouragement from professionals.

The same year, Margo secured her first real directing job with a community theater in the small California town of Ojai. After a year with the Ojai Community Players, she had a chance to travel around the world as a companion and secretary to a wealthy woman. How could she pass up this opportunity?

Margo used the fabulous year-long trip to learn more about the theater. She saw plays in Japan, China, India, England and France. She went to the theater every evening that her ship was in a foreign port. She visited nearly every large city in the world. But Margo had never before been to New York City—the center of American theater activities.

At the end of her trip, as Margo's ship finally entered New York harbor one fall evening in 1935, Margo saw the lights of the great City for the first time. As soon as she got off the ship, she headed for Broadway.

"The theatrical air was exhilarating, and it filled my lungs," she said. She knew she had to return someday to direct her own play.

While she had been abroad, Margo had heard about a government program called the Federal Theater. America was still in the grip of the 1930s' Depression, and many writers, actors and theater workers were unemployed. The government sponsored productions all over the country in an effort to put them back to work. Margo decided to go back to Texas and help with the program there.

She became assistant director at the Houston Federal Theater, co-sponsored by the Houston Recreation Department. But the program lasted only a few months.

Undaunted by failure, Margo went abroad again, this time to see the Moscow Art Theater Festival, which she covered in a series of articles for the *Houston Chronicle* newspaper. She also visited Berlin, Warsaw, London and Paris.

When she returned to Houston, her previous work with the recreation department helped Margo get a job teaching playground directors how to put on children's plays. It wasn't what she wanted to do, but she thought it might lead to something else.

What Margo really wanted was a theater of her own.

Margo asked the recreation department if she could use a small building to stage a dramatic production. When she got permission, she announced in the newspaper that the Houston Community Players planned to stage Oscar Wilde's play *The Importance of Being Earnest.*

It was a bold move by Margo. At the time there was no group called the Houston Com-

Margo Jones read at least one play every day. She developed an uncanny ability to recognize talented new playwrights.

53

munity Players. She made up the name and hoped she could create the Community Players if enough people showed up to try out for parts in the play. Now, she waited nervously to see if anyone would come the first day of tryouts.

Margo was lucky. Nine people showed up, and there were nine parts in the play. The show could go on. She could direct her first play independently! She charged 25 cents admission, and the play ran two nights in December 1936. It even got a favorable review in the newspaper. The Houston Community Players was born!

Margo decided to make the Community Players her full-time job. She believed she could sell enough season tickets at $2 each to pay her salary and production costs. She and her band of actors managed to bring in enough ticket sales to keep going. By the end of her second season, the Houston Recreation Department liked Margo's work so much that they put her on the payroll. Margo had proven that her theater could succeed.

"My ambition was to make the Houston Community Players the most exciting theater in America," Margo said.

By the early 1940s, the Houston Community Players had grown from those first nine actors to nearly 600 participants. It had produced more than sixty plays and had acquired $15,000 worth of equipment.

This is a diagram of the theater-in-the-round staging in Margo Jones's Dallas theater. In the close quarters, everyone in the audience had an excellent view and could almost reach out and touch the actors.

But Margo had a problem. Her theater building in Houston was too hot to use during the summer, and air-conditioning was too expensive to consider. She could put on her plays successfully in the winter, but how could she establish a year-round theater season like New York had?

After attending a theater conference in Washington D.C., Margo had an inspiration. At the conference she had seen a play performed on the floor of a hotel ballroom. There was no elevated stage, simply a performance area roped off and surrounded by seats for the audience. It was theater-in-the-round, similar to the staging sometimes used hundreds of years earlier in theatrical productions.

Why not try this theater-in-the-round out in Houston? All Margo had to do was convince a Houston hotel to let her use one of its air-conditioned meeting rooms for her plays. She could be in business for the summer! Margo was a very persuasive woman and this was one of the many times she got her way. Her group performed six plays in a cool hotel ballroom that hot Houston summer.

World War II ended Margo's Houston Community Players. Many of the actors and production crew members joined the Army and left Houston for the war effort. Margo left Houston, too. She became a drama teacher at the University of Texas at Austin.

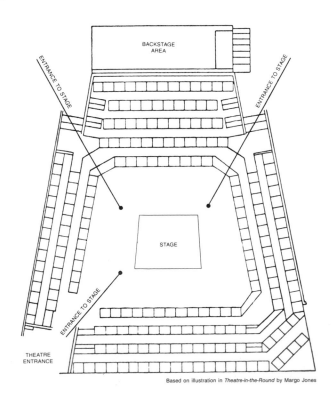

Based on illustration in *Theatre-in-the-Round* by Margo Jones

Because of the success of her productions in Houston, and her growing reputation as a drama teacher, Margo was also invited to direct several plays by unknown playwrights during the war. She staged Tennessee Williams's and Donald Windham's play *You Touched Me* in Cleveland, Ohio, and Pasadena, California. But the war years were generally slow for Margo. And they gave her time to nurture her expanding theatrical dreams.

Margo wanted to develop a theater outside of New York — not with an amateur company like she had in Houston, but with a company of full-time, paid professional actors and technicians. She wanted young actors and playwrights to have a chance to find work. And she wanted people all over the country to see top-notch professional theater.

She found out that many other theater people shared her dream. The country needed theaters outside of New York. Actors and playwrights needed the jobs. Everyone agreed with Margo, but nobody was doing anything about it! It was easy enough to dream, but hard to make the dreams come true.

"We dream beautifully, but what are we doing about it? Why do we keep talking?" Margo asked.

Enough talk! Margo decided she'd take some action. Her new motto became, "Put up or shut up."

Margo had no money, no building, no actors, no plays. She had nothing except her dream and determination. But Margo developed a plan to secure a beautiful theater building, the best actors, quality manuscripts — nothing less than the best!

After World War II, she told the *Dallas Morning News* drama critic about her plan.

"Why not here?" he asked. Dallas was a thriving, growing city. People were making money, and they were interested in bringing more cultural events to the city. Dallas needed a good theater. Word about Margo's plan began circulating in Dallas. Many people encouraged her.

But Margo now faced a turning point. She needed time — time to research finances, scripts, personnel and available theater buildings. She estimated it would take about a year before she could open a first-class theater. But she had no money. She wrote the Rockefeller Foundation, an organization that gives money to worthy projects, and asked for enough money to travel for a year, "to visit as many theaters as possible . . . to watch the best designers, lighting people, directors and all technicians at work . . . to talk to the young playwrights. I want to collect new scripts and read at least three plays a day during the year of work."

Margo gave the Rockefeller Foundation a list of things she wanted to accomplish at the end of one year. She wanted:
- a theater building, ready to open
- a staff of twenty
- funds to pay the staff
- new scripts, new ideas and "new dreams enough to keep us all busy for one hundred years."

"I can dream, can't I?" Margo asked.

Margo put her best persuasive powers to work in the plan she submitted to the Rockefeller Foundation. She told them she wanted a theater that would enable Dallasites to say 20 years from now, "My children have lived in a town where they could see the best plays of the world presented in a beautiful and fine way."

The Rockefeller Foundation believed in Margo and in Margo's dream and granted her the money for her year of travel and development of a new theater for Dallas.

Three months into the year of travel, another opportunity came along for Margo. Her friend, the young playwright Tennessee Williams, was going to have his first play produced on Broadway. He wanted Margo to co-direct it. Margo had guided some of his early plays through production, and Tennessee felt Margo was the only one who could insure a Broadway success of his play, *The Glass Menagerie.*

Margo decided she would do it.

The Glass Menagerie was a Broadway blockbuster. It made Tennessee Williams famous. And it made Margo Jones one of the most respected theatrical directors in America. Margo could have stayed on Broadway forever. Playwrights and producers offered her plays to direct. Actors and actresses were eager to work with her.

But Margo had not forgotten her dream for a great theater for Dallas. She returned. But it was different now.

Margo was no longer an unknown. She was a Broadway success. People in Dallas recognized

Far left. Margo Jones's Broadway production of *The Glass Menagerie* by Tennessee Williams established her national reputation. In this scene from the play, Laura is absorbed in a private moment with her small glass animals.

Above. Well-known stars, like Ingrid Bergman shown here with Margo, were eager to act under Margo's direction. Miss Bergman performed in Margo's Broadway production of *Joan of Lorraine* in 1946.

Left. Each New Year's Eve, Margo changed the name of her theater to match the new year. Here, Theatre '52 became Theatre '53.

that Margo was giving them a golden opportunity to have quality theater there. They began contributing funds for her theater. A civic-minded couple contributed $10,000. Margo set up a board of directors and officially incorporated as "Dallas Theater, Inc." After her success in Houston, Margo decided to have a theater-in-the-round in Dallas, too.

All she needed was a theater building. On the Texas State Fairgrounds, she found a small exhibits building which was leased to the Gulf Oil Corporation. It was air-conditioned and adaptable to theater-in-the-round. She persuaded Gulf to allow her to use it free of charge as long as she paid the utility bill. When Gulf's lease later ran out, the company sold it to her for a nominal fee.

Once Margo had her building, she took off like a rocket. She immediately planned a 10-week season of five plays. She knew exactly which productions she wanted to stage—four new plays and one well-loved classic. The season would open June 3, 1947—only eight weeks away!

Margo flew to New York. In three weeks' time, she bought the rights to four plays, hired a business manager and a company of eight actors. Meanwhile, back in Dallas, the staff was printing tickets, mailing advertising flyers, renovating the theater building, and purchasing technical equipment. Everyone operated at a frenzied pace.

Margo gave the actors railroad tickets for the trip from New York to Dallas, and they arrived three weeks before opening night.

In a promotional brochure, Margo proudly announced to the People of Dallas:

Opening June 3
Theatre '47
10 Weeks of Summer Season
of
Theatre in the Round
Air Conditioned Gulf Oil Theatre . . . Fair Park

The season started slowly, but soon crowds began to attend. By the third production, Margo knew her theater was a hit. "As a whole, it was a fantastically successful first season," she said.

Dallas responded to Margo, grateful to her for putting Dallas on the map in the world of

Margo Jones Collection, Dallas Public Library

Above. Actor Charles Laughton attended Theatre '54 with Margo.
Right. Margo, second from right, put her cast through rigorous rehearsals for Theatre '49.

theater. She succeeded in proving that a professional, innovative theater company could thrive in a city outside New York.

Theatre '47 ran for 10 weeks. When 1948 began, Margo changed the name to match the year. It was a tradition she would continue each year. Theatre '48 ran for 20 weeks. Theatre '49 and Theatre '50 each ran for 30 weeks. The people of Dallas flocked to see the biggest names in the acting business. And they came to see world premieres of plays that, in time, the rest of the country would see.

Margo had an uncanny ability to select good scripts and forge them into fine productions. In her very first season she presented *Summer and Smoke* by Tennessee Williams. It became so popular that it was produced on Broadway the next year. Another play of that first season, *Farther Off from Heaven*, William Inge's first play, was eventually made into a movie entitled *Dark at the Top of the Stairs*.

In 1954, Margo came across a script that she loved. It was called *Inherit the Wind* and was a story based on the famous Scopes Trial of 1925. The actual trial had inflamed the nation; it had pitted two famous American lawyers against each other in a dramatic courtroom battle. Clarence Darrow and William Jennings Bryan argued over whether the theory of evolution should be taught in the public schools. The state of Tennessee had arrested and brought to trial a young public

59

school teacher named John Scopes for teaching evolution, contrary to the state law. Bryan argued Tennessee's position, and Darrow argued for Scopes's right to teach evolution in the school. The Scopes Trial was a dramatic, emotion-filled event in America's history.

Inherit the Wind by Jerome Lawrence and Robert Lee was a re-enactment of that famous trial. The play thrilled Margo, because all of the action took place in a courtroom. It was emotional and suspenseful, full of intellectual ideas and dramatic action.

To Margo, it brought back all of the excitement she had felt as a child when she watched her father's trials in the courtroom at Livingston. It took her back to the beginnings of her dream to create that kind of drama on stage.

Margo threw herself into the production of *Inherit the Wind.* It premiered at her theater January 10, 1955.

Opening night, Margo sat backstage at the top of the stairs and watched. The cast and crew were nervous. The subject of the play was still controversial. The audience was quiet. Then it was over.

The crowd erupted with thundering applause.

"When Margo came down and told us it was wonderful, we knew we had a hit," one actress in the performance recalled.

And it was a hit. Perhaps Margo's biggest. The play went to Broadway after Dallas and became a long-running sensation. And it was made into a classic movie in 1960 starring Spencer Tracy in the Clarence Darrow role.

This dramatic scene was from *Inherit the Wind*, Margo's last, and perhaps greatest, Dallas theater production. No other director recognized the excellence of the play until Margo produced it for Theatre '55. The play went on to a long life as a Broadway hit and, later, as a feature film.

Inherit the Wind was one of Margo's last triumphs.

On July 24, 1955, Margo was the victim of a strange accident. She had fallen asleep on the floor of her apartment and inhaled the deadly fumes of a cleaning fluid that had been used to clean her carpet that day. Margo, 42 years old, died two weeks later.

The theater world was shocked. Dallas was saddened. Her friends and associates were grief-stricken.

The great playwright Thornton Wilder called Margo "a builder, an explorer, a mixer of truth and magic."

Her loss was keenly felt. Margo's Dallas theater did not survive. Without her drive and dedication, it lasted only four years after her death. But Margo's influence knew no boundary. Theater lovers established regional theaters all across the United States. Many of them were patterned after Margo's Dallas theater.

In her short life, Margo realized her dreams. She experienced the fame, the glamour of opening night, the opportunity to work with the best actors and actresses of her time, and the chance to direct her own way. She pursued her dream, and she loved making it come true.

Once, she told an aspiring dramatist what she considered to be the secret of her success.

"You must have a capacity for a tremendous amount of hard work, and a joy in doing so," she said.

Margo Jones had both. A capacity for hard work. And a joy in carrying it out.

Margo Jones was the first director and producer to establish a highly acclaimed professional theater company in Texas.

62

Clara Driscoll had everything: beauty, brains and money. That would have been enough for most women. But Clara Driscoll also had compassion, generosity and plain good sense. And using all these qualities, she made a major impact on Texas and its people.

Daughter of a millionaire South Texas rancher, Clara lived a life of independence, glamour and excitement. By the time she was 18 years old, she had traveled around the world and visited every country in Europe.

When she was just 22 years old, she wrote checks to purchase land around the Alamo. She thus saved the monument from commercial exploitation or even destruction. From then on, Clara was known as the "Savior of the Alamo."

But she didn't stop there. Clara became just as well known throughout the country as an author, playwright, politician, diplomat and businesswoman. Like a versatile actress in a one-woman show, she filled every role she stepped into with dramatic success.

Philanthropy — the effort to increase the wellbeing of others through charitable donations — became Clara's hallmark. Beginning with her purchase of the Alamo grounds on behalf of all Texans, she continued to use her wealth to benefit others. If she believed in a cause, a political candidate or an organization, she contributed her money to help in any way it could.

True, Clara had inherited her wealth. But she alone decided how to spend it. She could have squandered the family fortune. Instead, she enlarged it and spent it wisely. Texans today continue to profit from her generosity. This is Clara Driscoll's story.

Savior of the Alamo
CLARA DRISCOLL
(1881–1945)

Clara Driscoll grew up in the rough and tumble world of Texas ranching. Born to a wealthy family in the South Texas town of St. Mary's in 1881, she absorbed the spirit of adventure around her.

Clara had striking features: dark red hair, fiery eyes and creamy skin. Her delicate beauty, however, did not dictate her behavior.

As a girl, she learned to do almost everything the cowboys did. She could hit a bullseye squarely with rifle or revolver. She could sit straight in the saddle on the fastest of horses. She was even an expert with a lariat.

Plainly, she had spunk. According to one story, she once single-handedly cornered a group of cattle thieves on the ranch. They quickly regretted their crime when they stared into the barrel of Clara's gun.

Clara loved the customs and culture of South Texas. She danced to Mexican folk music and spoke Spanish like a native.

For all her love of Texas, Clara spent much of her childhood out of the state. Her father, Robert Driscoll, had amassed a fortune by the time she was born, and he was always generous with Clara and her brother, Robert Jr. Clara lived a very cosmopolitan childhood. She attended the finest girls' schools in New York and Paris. There she studied German, French, literature and the arts. Between school terms, she traveled around the world with her mother.

Despite her worldly travels, Clara's roots ran deep in Texas. When she returned from an extended Spanish vacation at the turn of the century, she learned that the great symbol of Texas liberty — the Alamo — was nearly in ruins. Buildings blocked its view. Clara was indignant!

Although the state of Texas owned the crumbling chapel of the Alamo, the rest of the historical buildings and property had fallen into commercial hands — namely, the Hugo and Schmeltzer grocery and liquor business.

To make matters worse, the Hugo and Schmeltzer property was up for sale. An eastern business wanted to buy the Alamo property for $75,000 and build a hotel on the site. Once built, the hotel would stand almost on top of the historic chapel.

During her travels abroad, Clara had observed how Europeans valued and preserved their historical buildings and monuments. Why didn't Texans?

Clara thought they should, especially a structure as historically significant as the Alamo.

She first expressed her concern for preserving the Alamo in a letter to the editor of the *San Antonio Express* in 1901:

> *It is our Alamo . . . and how do we treat it? How can we expect others to attach the importance to it that it so well deserves, when we Texans, who live with its shadow, are so careless of its existence? . . . Today the Alamo should stand out, free and clear. All the unsightly obstructions should be torn away.*

Clara undertook a personal crusade to save the Alamo. She joined the Daughters of the Republic of Texas (DRT), a group also eager to save the Alamo. The DRT was founded in 1891 with the purpose of preserving Texas's historic structures. Saving the Alamo was their biggest challenge.

Clara and other DRT members decided that the only way to save the Alamo was to buy the property themselves. But how were they to raise the $25,000 down payment?

They tried a little bit of everything. They held fundraising benefits and bazaars. They solicited money from interested school children and teachers around the state. They issued printed pleas for funds.

Clara spoke to legislators in Austin to enlist their support. She sent letters to newspapers to plead the Alamo cause.

But the energetic efforts of Clara and the DRT fell far short of their financial goal. By 1903, they

When Clara Driscoll began her crusade to save the Alamo, the mission was already overshadowed by the Hugo & Schmeltzer warehouse. Plans were being made to build a multi-storied hotel on the site. That could have meant the end for the Alamo.

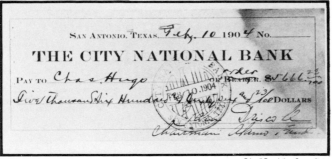

After a statewide fundraising campaign failed to produce enough money to purchase the Alamo property, Clara Driscoll decided to buy it herself. She wrote a total of nearly $75,000 in checks to Hugo & Schmeltzer in payment for the Alamo grounds. And she gave the property to the Daughters of the Republic of Texas. Today the Alamo stands as an imposing historical structure. It attracts more visitors each year than any other historic site in Texas.

had raised less than $6,000 toward the $75,000 they needed to buy the property. Time was running out. Then Clara made a decision.

Clara went to see her father for advice. She asked him if he thought $75,000 was a fair asking price for the Alamo.

"Yes," Mr. Driscoll said. It was a reasonable sum and the terms were fair.

But he asked, "Do you know anyone who will throw that much money away on the slim chance that the state may sometime repay it?"

"Yes," answered Clara. "I know such a person."

"Who?" her father asked incredulously.

"Myself. I have the money, and I don't care whether the state repays me or not."

"Yes, Clara," her father said. "You have your own bank account and far be it from me to tell you how to use your money. But are you sure that is what you want to do?"

"I am absolutely sure," she replied.

"Then, my dear, I'll see that you have enough in your account to cover the $75,000."

Immediately Clara called on the men who owned the Alamo property and agreed to buy it for $75,000. Then she wrote a check for a $25,000 down payment on the spot. She agreed to pay the $50,000 balance in five yearly installments of $10,000, plus six per cent interest.

She spelled out in the agreement: "This property is purchased by Clara Driscoll for the use and benefit of the Daughters of the Republic of Texas, and is to be used by them for the purpose of making a park about the Alamo, and for no other purpose whatever."

The news sent shockwaves throughout Texas and the nation.

A 22-year-old woman had bought the Alamo!

Overnight, Clara became a celebrity. Newspapers around the country printed articles about her. The name Clara Driscoll appeared in headline after headline. Everyone asked, "Who is this young woman who goes around writing checks to save the Alamo?"

Texans hailed Clara as the "Savior of the Alamo." She was thrust into the spotlight of national publicity, and she loved it.

What would have happened to the Alamo if Clara had not acted? Perhaps business buildings would have eventually surrounded the chapel. The Alamo chapel itself might have been

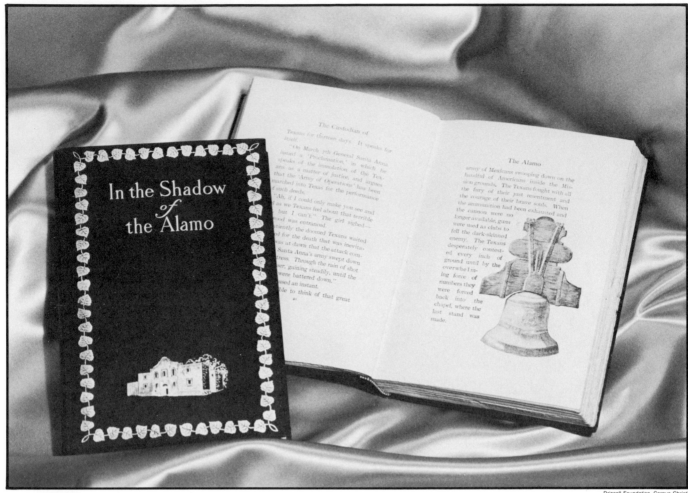

The Alamo captured Clara's creative imagination as well as her Texas pride. In 1906 she published *In the Shadow of the Alamo*, a book of short stories set in San Antonio.

demolished. Texans would have had neither the beautiful park nor the monument to Texas heroes that exists today.

The $75,000 may not have been a great loss to Clara's massive fortune. But the destruction of the Alamo would have been a great loss to the people of Texas. It would have also been an immense personal loss to Clara, who had put her heart and soul into the campaign to save it.

Clara's action created so much publicity that the state legislature addressed the Alamo question. Legislators overwhelmingly approved a bill directing the state to pay for the preservation of the Alamo. Texas reimbursed Clara $65,000 of the money she had paid for the property.

The Alamo cause was only one in a long series of adventures in Clara's life.

Infused with the success of her Alamo victory, Clara immediately launched her writing career.

She published a romantic novel of South Texas called *Girl of la Gloria* in 1905. The story depicts the Mexican-American customs and characters she became familiar with as a child.

In 1906, she published a book of short stories, *In the Shadow of the Alamo.* That same year she wrote a comic opera, *Mexicana.* It enjoyed a successful run on Broadway in New York City.

These literary feats kept the name of Clara Driscoll in the national press.

In July 1906, Clara embarked on another adventure. She married Texas newspaperman Hal Sevier. They had met when he was a legislator, and she was campaigning for the Alamo cause.

The couple moved to New York and built a luxurious home on Long Island, next to the estate of former President Theodore Roosevelt. Clara and Hal relished the glamour and excitement of New York City, and they threw lavish parties. Clara, always the patriotic Texan, helped start the Texas Club for Texans living in New York.

Following the death of Clara's father in 1914, the Seviers returned to Texas. They moved to

Austin, where Hal founded the *Austin-American* newspaper. On the banks of the Colorado River, they built their dream house and called it "Laguna Gloria"—heavenly lagoon.

The Seviers became the darling couple of the political and social life of Austin. Clara was active in club work, serving as president of the Austin Garden Club and the Daughters of the Republic of Texas.

Her leadership role didn't stop there. In 1928, Clara was elected Democratic national committeewoman from Texas. She again emerged in the national spotlight. Clara remained committeewoman for a record 16 years.

Perhaps she acquired her taste for politics during her legislative lobbying for the Alamo cause. Perhaps it just came naturally. Acquaintances said she loved a good argument. Whatever the source, Clara became an accomplished politician in the difficult world of national politics. She was an unflagging compaigner for the candidates she supported and even contributed $250,000 toward Vice President John Nance Garner's unsuccessful presidential bid.

"Politicians learned to respect her," wrote *Time* magazine about Clara Driscoll. "She could drink, battle, cuss and connive with the best of them, outspend practically all of them."

In 1929, Clara met another challenge. Her brother Robert died, leaving her the sole heir to the huge Driscoll business and civic empire. Could Clara direct one of Texas's largest estates?

At the time, few women anywhere had a position of such wealth and power. Some women ran their own businesses. But Clara would be running dozens.

True to character, Clara accepted the challenge and approached her new responsibilities with zest. She and Hal moved to Corpus Christi, the center of the Driscoll empire.

Clara assumed control of 100,000 acres of land, 16 oil wells, three gas wells, three cotton gins and numerous real estate holdings in Corpus Christi.

She became the president and sole owner of Corpus Christi Bank and Trust Company and the largest stockholder of the Corpus Christi National Bank.

At the height of the Great Depression in the 1930s, when business after business went broke,

the value of the Driscoll estate almost doubled under Clara's management. She wheeled and dealed and made million-dollar agreements. Clara's business successes were astounding. She became one of the most influential people in South Texas. Her legend grew.

Still, when she was asked to describe her occupation, Clara replied, "I am a cattlewoman." Indeed, she still loved to relax while watching the cattle graze at her childhood ranch home.

In 1933, Hal Sevier was appointed ambassador to Chile by President Franklin D. Roosevelt. Clara and Hal greeted the life in South America with enthusiasm. But this journey did not produce the joy or success of their previous adventures.

Political turmoil and personal problems plagued Hal and Clara in Chile. Rumors circulated that Clara, not Hal, had taken over many of the ambassadorial duties and that Hal was in poor health. In 1935, two years short of the end of his term, Hal Sevier resigned his post.

The Seviers returned to Texas, then separated later that year. Clara divorced Hal in 1937. Afterwards, she petitioned the court to allow her to take back her family name. She became officially known as Mrs. Clara Driscoll.

Clara was now 56 years old. For the rest of her life, she endowed the clubs and causes that she had always believed in and supported—historic preservation, politics and the arts.

Clara never forgot her beloved Alamo. She donated money for repairs and paid the caretaker's salary for several years so the public would not have to pay a visitor's fee.

She gave the state $65,000 to buy land around the Alamo to convert into gardens.

In 1938, she lent $92,000 to the Texas Federation of Women's Clubs to help pay the debt on the headquarters building in Austin. One year later, she converted the loan to a gift.

She turned over her elegant Laguna Gloria mansion in Austin and its naturally beautiful grounds to the Texas Fine Arts Association in 1943. Today, it is a popular art museum.

One of Clara's last business enterprises was a boon to the wartime economy of Corpus Christi. She built a $3.5 million hotel during the early years of World War II, when little building was being undertaken anywhere in the country.

Clara gave her Austin mansion, Laguna Gloria, to the Texas Fine Arts Association in 1943. Today it houses a popular modern art museum.

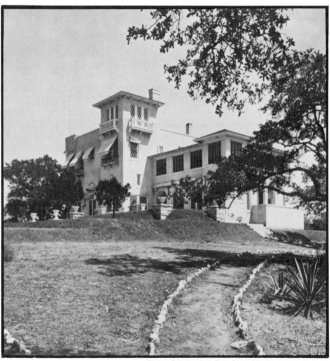

She named it for her brother, Robert Driscoll. The luxury, high-rise hotel — at that time the largest and most modern in the whole Southwest — greatly enhanced the tourist industry of Corpus Christi when it opened in 1941.

Clara died suddenly on July 17, 1945. She was 64 years old.

The honorary pallbearers at her funeral included the biggest names in Texas politics at the time: former Vice-President John Nance Garner, U.S. House Speaker Sam Rayburn, future President Lyndon Johnson, Senator Tom Connally, Congressman Richard Kleberg and others. Hundreds of mourners filed by as her body lay in state in the Alamo.

Clara Driscoll could have been satisfied with just being known as the savior of the Alamo. In-

Clara participated in national Democratic party politics and actively supported Franklin Roosevelt's first campaign for President in 1932. In 1933, President Roosevelt appointed Hal Sevier, Clara's husband, as Ambassador to Chile. Hal and Clara, seated at front center, ran the U.S. Embassy there for two years.

71

stead, she also excelled in the worlds of business, politics and philanthropy.

And yet, unbelievably, Clara's greatest gift came after her death. In her will she directed that her vast family fortune be used to establish a hospital for the crippled and diseased children of South Texas. At the time of her death, many poor children in South Texas suffered from polio or tuberculosis. No specialized treatment was available. Since its completion in 1953, the Driscoll Foundation Children's Hospital in Corpus Christi has served as a model for other facilities throughout the country. Clara's hospital has relieved the suffering of more than one million young Texans.

Clara Driscoll's legacy lives on. She left her family fortune for the establishment of the Driscoll Foundation Children's Hospital to treat crippled and ill South Texas children. The hospital is located in Corpus Christi and has treated more than one million young patients.

All her life, Clara gave money generously to help others. Yet it is still the act of saving the Alamo for which she is most often remembered.

A bronze tablet on the walls of the Alamo ensures that Clara will live in the memory of all Texans:

Lest We Forget
Title to the Alamo Mission property
Acquired by her Efforts and Personal Fortune
Was Conveyed by
Clara Driscoll
To the State of Texas
September 5, 1905
That the Sacred Shrine be Saved
From the encroachments of Commercialism
And Stand through Eternity
A Monument Incomparable
To the Immortal Heroes
Who Died that Texas might not Perish.

Driscoll Foundation, Corpus Christi

JOVITA IDAR

LEONOR VILLEGAS
DE MAGNON

One of the first political revolutions of the 20th century took place in Mexico — Texas's great neighbor to the south. From 1910 until the 1940s, Mexico was in turmoil. For the first ten years, bloody civil war pitted various revolutionary armies, composed of farmers and workers, against government troops. One revolutionary leader after another was assassinated. One government after another failed to impose stability. Even after most of the battles ended, the struggle to fulfill the dreams of the Revolution went on for another 22 years.

But the Mexican Revolution was not just a series of battles — it became a set of beliefs.

At the center of the revolution were deeply held ideals and demands for justice, equality, land reform, economic opportunity, religious freedom and independence from any foreign control. The ideas were heady — even intoxicating. And those ideas spilled across the Mexican border into Texas just like the thousands of refugees who fled the battles and bloodshed.

Nowhere did the events and ideas of the Mexican Revolution have a greater impact on Americans than on the people who lived along the border. Most border-area residents were of Mexican ancestry, and many had relatives still in Mexico. Residents of Laredo, Brownsville, El Paso, and even San Antonio 150 miles to the north, kept up with the progress of events and ideas in Mexico. Some got used to seeing various revolutionary leaders who stayed in their cities for brief periods of exile from the turmoil in Mexico. American citizens even watched some of the battles of the revolution which were fought in border areas. All they had to do was stand on a hill on the American side of the Rio Grande to watch revolutionary armies fight the Mexican government troops.

Two Texas women were particularly affected by the events they saw. Jovita Idar and Leonor Villegas de Magnon lived in Laredo, and each in her own way used the ideas and events of the revolution to help others.

Leonor Villegas de Magnon organized La Cruz Blanca (The White Cross) to provide disaster relief and medical aid to soldiers and civilians injured during the revolution. La Cruz Blanca became an honored organization on both sides of the border.

Jovita Idar used her fiery pen and talent as a writer to spread the progressive ideas of the revolution among Mexican-Americans in Texas. Her writings and community work helped to plant seeds for Mexican-American civil rights efforts which bore fruit more than 40 years later.

Each woman took risks to do what she believed was right. Neither flinched from the physical dangers of battle, nor from the attempts by those in power to intimidate them. They were brave leaders during difficult times. This is their story.

74

Photos courtesy of Jovita Lopez, San Antonio and Leonor M. Grubbs, Houston

Women of a Revolution

JOVITA IDAR
(1885–1946)

LEONOR VILLEGAS DE MAGNON
(1876–1955)

W hat is unfairness?

That is a hard question to answer if you are a little girl.

Jovita Idar's father tried to help her answer that question. In the early 1900s, Nicasio Idar published a newspaper, called *La Cronica*, in Laredo, and he wrote about unfairness all the time.

He believed that Anglo-Americans in Laredo—and all of South Texas—did not treat Mexican-Americans fairly. He thought it was wrong for Mexican-Americans, who were, after all, American citizens, to be denied opportunities because of who their ancestors were, or where they came from, or what language they spoke, or what color their skin was. Mr. Idar's hero was Abraham Lincoln, and like Lincoln, he pursued his cause fiercely when he believed it to be right. When he saw something that he thought was unfair in Laredo, he wrote about it in his newspaper—and talked to young Jovita and her brothers about it.

It was unfair for most of the good jobs to be closed to Mexican-Americans, his newspaper articles said.

It was wrong for the police and judges to treat Mexican-Americans differently from Anglo-Americans.

It was harmful for the schools of Mexican-American children to be inferior to the schools of the Anglo children.

It was humiliating to see signs in public places which said, "No Mexicans Allowed."

And on and on, he wrote.

Jovita began to learn what unfairness really meant. And she grew up believing that Texans of Mexican ancestry often did not have the same kinds of opportunities that Anglo-Texans had. That made her angry. So she decided that, like her father, she would try to do something about the problems that seemed so unfair to her.

But how?

What could she do? She loved to read. She loved to write poetry. Perhaps if she became a teacher she could do the things she loved and still help the Mexican-American children.

So Jovita studied at the Holding Institute in Laredo and earned a teaching certificate in 1903.

Then she began teaching in the little South Texas town of Ojuelos. But like most teachers who taught in schools for Mexican-American children, Jovita did not have enough textbooks for her students. She did not have enough pencils or paper. Some days, when all the pupils were present, she did not have enough desks or chairs for them to sit in. On cold days, there was no heat.

And there was nothing Jovita could do about it. The Anglo-Americans controlled the school taxing authority and they would not provide more money for the Mexican-American schools.

My teaching is not helping enough, Jovita thought. I must do more.

So Jovita quit her teaching job and went back home to Laredo to write for her father's newspaper. Helping Texas citizens of Mexican ancestry became the most important thing in the world to Jovita. And she set out to do whatever she could to make their lives better. Perhaps her writing would help more than her teaching.

She wrote impassioned articles arguing for the rights of Mexican-Americans. And her passion turned to outrage over one particular incident in Laredo.

A 14-year-old Mexican-American boy was arrested for murder. In the American system of justice, an individual is entitled to a trial by jury. The jury determines guilt or innocence. But the judicial system did not have a chance to work for this young boy. Before he could be brought to trial, a mob of Anglo citizens kidnapped him from the police, beat him to death, tied his body behind a buggy and dragged him through the streets of Laredo.

Jovita and her family were furious. They decided that they must do more than merely write about these kinds of injustices. They must take action! The year was 1911.

At the same time across the border, the Mexican Revolution was underway. The people of Mexico had thrown out a corrupt government that was unresponsive to their needs. Now, the revolutionaries demanded justice and oppor-

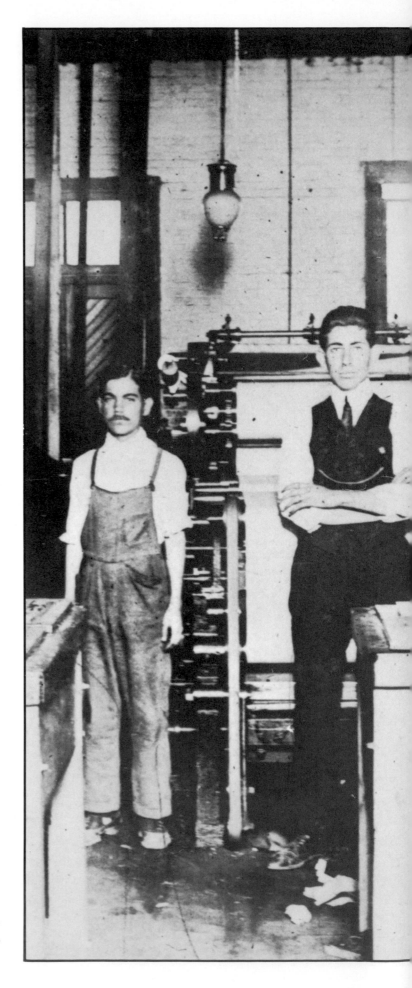

Jovita Idar, second from right, was a noted writer for her father's newspaper *La Cronica* and for *El Progresso*, whose print shop is shown here in 1914.

Jovita Lopez, San Antonio

tunity. Jovita and her family publicly sided with the revolutionaries against the Mexican government.

The excitement of events in Mexico—and recent incidents in Laredo—caused Jovita and her family to take a very daring step in Texas.

They issued a call in 1911, for Mexican-Americans to meet together in Laredo to decide what to do about their problems. It was the first meeting of its kind in Texas for citizens of Mexican ancestry. The group met in September to discuss education, criminal justice and labor. They called their meeting *El Primer Congreso Mexicanista* (The First Mexican Congress).

Jovita especially wanted women to attend the Congress. She knew that they were concerned about these issues, but she also knew that many were afraid to speak out in public. Jovita urged them to come to the Congress anyway.

And they did. Many Mexican-American women entered the public political arena for the first time when they attended the Congress. There, they spoke out against violence to Mexican-Americans and for better educational opportunities for women and children.

One month after the Congress, Jovita and several other Laredo women took another bold step—they started their own organization, *La Liga Femenil Mexicanista* (The League of Mexican Women). The women elected Jovita as their first president.

The League brought new pride and a sense of accomplishment to the Mexican-American women. For their first project, they provided free elementary school classes for poor Laredo children. They later collected food, clothing and school supplies for poor families. They also held regular study sessions so that the women could educate themselves.

At last, Jovita felt she was really doing something significant to help her people.

Then one day in 1913, the Mexican Revolution came very close to Jovita and her family. Revolutionary soldiers attacked Nuevo Laredo, Laredo's sister city, just across the Rio Grande in Mexico. The gunfire, explosions and burning homes created panic. Mothers and fathers grabbed their small children and ran through the streets, trying to find a haven from the gunfire. Soldiers fired at anything that moved. All was chaos.

In Laredo, the sounds of the battle were frightening. Cries and screams of children could be heard, along with the gunfire. People needed help.

What could Jovita do?

Her answer came with a call from her friend Leonor Villegas de Magnon, who was recruiting women to give medical aid to the injured.

Would Jovita cross the Rio Grande to help?

Without hesitation, Jovita said, "Yes."

Then Jovita quickly crossed the river to Nuevo Laredo and entered the battle in progress. Jovita, Leonor and a small group of women volunteers pulled wounded soldiers from the streets and took them to the hospital. Once at the hospital, they assisted physicians.

The fighting went on for hours, and Jovita did everything she could to assist with the nursing of the wounded. The women kept going out into the streets to bring the wounded to safety. Bullets whizzed over their heads. But they kept on. They were exhausted—but they continued.

The services of the women proved invaluable. They saved hundreds of lives through their quick action. And once the battle in Nuevo Laredo was over, Leonor led the women to establish a new medical relief organization. It became known as *La Cruz Blanca* (The White Cross). It was similar to the American Red Cross. *La Cruz Blanca* volunteers wore armbands with the symbol of the white cross. They traveled into Mexico to assist the revolutionary army, and they cared for the wounded in battle after battle.

Jovita later became a war nurse for *La Cruz Blanca* and, with Leonor Villegas de Magnon, traveled in northern Mexico with the revolutionary army. Jovita's brother accompanied the women. For several months, they braved gunfire and primitive conditions to help the wounded. The experience strengthened Jovita's resolve to continue her writing and organizing.

Back in the United States, Jovita took up her pen again to promote her causes. She wrote for the Spanish-language newspaper, *El Progresso*. One incident put the newspaper—and Jovita—in opposition to the whole United States government.

The revolutionary battles along the Texas border frightened many United States citizens. They were afraid not only of the soldiers, but also of the ideas they represented. Poor people all over Mexico had taken up arms for better jobs, schools, farm lands and other personal and religious freedoms. Some Americans feared that poor Mexican-Americans on the United States side of the border might do the same thing. So they wanted the border cleared of all revolutionary activities.

In 1913, they persuaded United States President Woodrow Wilson to send U.S. troops to the Texas-Mexico border. *El Progresso* printed an editorial criticizing President Wilson's action.

The United States Army was outraged at the criticism. And the Texas Rangers decided to shut down the newspaper that dared to criticize the President.

The Rangers rushed through the streets of Laredo intent upon boarding up the offices of *El Progresso*. But they got a shock when they approached the building.

Standing in the doorway was a small, attractive woman—not a band of revolutionaries!

It was Jovita. She had decided to remain in the newspaper office when she learned that the lawmen were on their way.

Jovita believed in freedom of the press. It was a right guaranteed by the United States Constitution.

She would not stop writing about her causes — even if the famous Texas Rangers threatened to arrest her.

The Rangers looked at Jovita.

Jovita stared back.

There was a long silence.

Then the Rangers backed away, not Jovita.

Something in her confident manner or determined expression must have told them that she was a woman whose strong beliefs would give her the strength to resist whatever she considered an injustice. And obviously, she considered the closing of *El Progresso* unjust. The Rangers did not want to harm Jovita.

Although Jovita won that particular day in 1913, the Rangers did succeed in closing *El Progresso* later. And Jovita went back to writing for her father's *La Cronica.* When her father died,

she and her brothers decided to continue the newspaper as they believed their father would have wished.

Jovita married Bartolo Juarez in 1917, and they moved to San Antonio. Some thought she might "settle down" now that she was married and 32 years old. But Jovita never gave up her desire to better the lives of Mexican-Americans. And she continued her work in San Antonio.

Jovita set up a free kindergarten for Mexican-American children. She worked in the Democratic party. She served as an interpreter between doctors and Spanish-speaking patients at the county hospital. She became co-editor of *El Heraldo Christiano*, the publication of the Rio Grande Conference of the Methodist Church. And she continued to speak out when she thought Mexican-Americans were treated unfairly.

Jovita died in 1946, when she was 61 years old. She had lived through a violent age — in Mexico and Texas. She spoke out on the issues. She risked her life to nurse battle-wounded soldiers and civilians. She never hesitated to do what she believed was right.

Jovita Idar, far left with members of her family, continued her efforts on behalf of Texas's Mexican-American citizens in San Antonio, where she worked as an interpreter for patients at the Robert B. Green County Hospital.

Jovita Lopez, San Antonio

LEONOR VILLEGAS DE MAGNON

When she was a little girl, her father called her *La Rebelde*, the rebel. The name stayed with her throughout her life.

Leonor Villegas de Magnon was a lively, intelligent child. When she made up her mind to do something, no one could stop her. And she didn't mind arguing about it!

Some fathers in the 1870s in Mexico might not have wanted their little girls to be so independent or willful. Girls and women were supposed to be passive and obedient. But Leonor's father admired her spirit. And he encouraged his daughter to develop her independence. He wanted her to have every advantage that men had, so he saw that she got a good education.

Even though it broke his heart to see his little *La Rebelde* leave home, he sent her to school in the United States. Then, when Leonor grew up, she married a United States citizen, Adolpho Magnon.

Leonor and Adolpho had three children and for a time lived in Mexico City. Leonor's father, who had moved across the Texas border to Laredo, died there in 1910. Leonor was heartbroken. She took her children to Laredo to attend her father's funeral. But after the funeral she found that she could not get back to Mexico.

Revolutionary fighting had started in Mexico while Leonor attended the funeral. It was too dangerous to try to return home to Mexico City. Adolpho wrote her to "stay put." She did so, reluctantly. She opened a kindergarten in her home to occupy her time.

Leonor could not ignore the events in Mexico, however. Neither could the other exiles from Mexico who found themselves in Laredo. They debated the ideas of the revolution and tried to think of ways they could get involved. Like many of the exiles, Leonor's sympathies were with the revolutionaries who had overthrown the corrupt government and were now trying to implement their hopes for a new system of justice for Mexico.

If Leonor had been a politician, she could have joined in the plots and intrigue going on around her.

If she had been a commander, she could have led troops into battle.

But women were not politicians or commanders in 1910, and Leonor could not lead the revolutionary action. That didn't stop her from getting involved.

She followed the news of the revolution avidly and began to formulate her opinions.

She found that many Laredo citizens shared her interest, including the influential Idar family who published the Spanish language newspaper, *La Cronica*. Leonor began writing for *La Cronica*, outlining the issues of the conflict in Mexico. She defended the revolutionary cause against the Mexican government.

Leonor became good friends with Jovita Idar, a *La Cronica* writer. Both were independent and outspoken. They shared many of the same ideals.

Early on the morning of March 17, 1913, Leonor got her chance for direct action.

The people of Laredo awakened to the sound of rifle shots and cannon fire. Nuevo Laredo, across the Rio Grande from Laredo, was under attack.

Leonor sat upright in bed. Immediately she realized a battle had erupted. This was it!

She jumped out of bed, dressed hurriedly and rushed outside. The streets were filled with screaming people fleeing the gunfire. Leonor fought her way through the crowd, bumping into those running away from the battle scene. But Leonor didn't want to run away. She wanted to help the revolutionaries.

Leonor grabbed the arms of women she knew.

"Come help the wounded," she cried. "We must help."

As she ran along, she persuaded women to follow her.

She called her friend Jovita Idar and urged her to go to Nuevo Laredo, where Leonor was making her way.

The women reached the battle-torn town and immediately went to work.

They dragged soldiers and civilians from the streets to safety. They took others to Nuevo Laredo's general hospital. They assisted physicians and nursed gunshot victims. They worked tirelessly and heroically.

After the battle was over, Leonor's small band of women nurses knew they had saved hundreds of lives because they had been on the scene to provide immediate assistance. Soldiers would have bled to death in the street if Leonor and the women had not been there.

Leonor decided to form the women into a permanent organization designed to provide medical relief during the Revolution. She named her organization *La Cruz Blanca* (The White Cross), hoping it would be simliar to the Red Cross which Clara Barton started in 1881 in America. The women began to organize for assistance at battle sites, gathering medical supplies and bandages. They didn't have to wait long to put them to use.

Nuevo Laredo came under attack again on New Year's Day in 1914. Leonor rounded up the *La Cruz Blanca* women. But this time they were unable to cross the river into Nuevo Laredo.

The fight lasted for hours, leaving many revolutionaries wounded and dying. Some were shot trying to get across the Rio Grande to safety in Laredo.

To give treatment to the soldiers who managed to cross the river, Leonor turned her home into a hospital. Nearly 100 men made it to Leonor's home. Her living room became an oper-

Leonor Villegas de Magnon, left, formed *La Cruz Blanca* in 1913 to provide medical relief to the casualties of the Mexican Revolution. Jovita Idar, right, joined her and other Mexican-American women in treating battle victims on both sides of the border.

Sra. Leono

curando el primer h

de los federales en la batalla de N.L

Marzo 17 - 1913

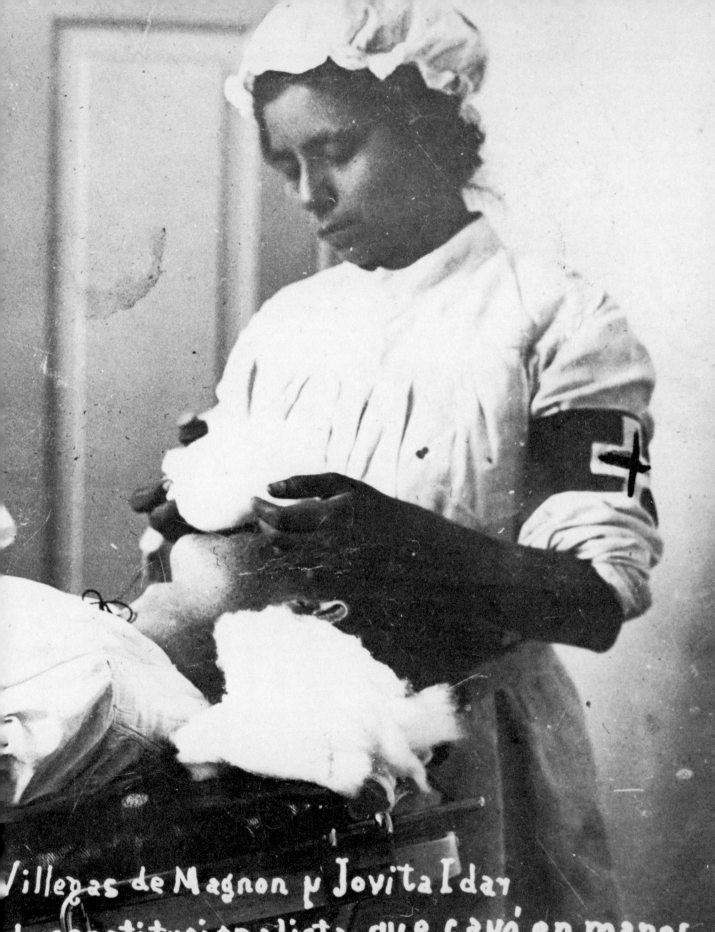

Villegas de Magnon y Jovita Idar

do constitucionalista que cayó en manos

edo, de las fuerzas de Jesus Carranza y Novoa

ating room. Local doctors and the women of *La Cruz Blanca* cared for the men day and night. Eventually, Leonor set up three emergency hospitals in Laredo.

By the end of January, about 50 men were well enough to leave Leonor's "hospital." But the rest still needed care. The United States Army ordered that the men be released from the hospital and sent to military prison. After all, they reasoned, these were Mexican revolutionaries on American soil.

Leonor refused to release them.

The army stationed soldiers outside Leonor's home.

But she still would not release the wounded revolutionaries.

She developed a plan. She got American citizens to come by her home, each bringing an extra set of clothes. Then, she dressed the wounded soldiers in the new clothes and discarded their bloody and dirty soldiers' garb.

When the revolutionary soldiers walked away from her house, the army couldn't tell who they were!

Leonor was able to get about 15 men safely past the army. But the most seriously wounded were unable to take advantage of Leonor's cleverness.

The U.S. Army finally took 37 of Leonor's patients into custody and put them into prison.

The army thought it had won.

Leonor decided otherwise. She believed that the men were innocent, that they had not committed any crime and that they should not be in prison! She hired a lawyer to argue the case for the soldiers' innocence. And she personally fired off letters to the Governor of Texas, a Texas

Jovita Idar, third from left, and Leonor Villegas de Magnon, far right, were honored by the Mexican government for their *La Cruz Blanca* service. Leonor received five medals for her war work.

Senator, the U.S. War Department and the U.S. Secretary of State.

She finally won. Secretary of State William Jennings Bryan ordered the prisoners' release.

Word of the courageous efforts of Leonor de Magnon and *La Cruz Blanca* in Laredo spread across the border deep into Mexico. When the revolutionary leader Venustiano Carranza heard about them, he urged the group to help him in Mexico. Leonor immediately telegraphed that she and 25 nurses were ready to join him. Jovita Idar was one of the nurses.

They joined Carranza's army at Cuidad Juarez, across the Rio Grande from El Paso. Throughout the year of 1914, Leonor's group braved wartime conditions to nurse the wounded in battle after battle. They risked their lives daily to provide support for the revolution. With each battle, they followed Carranza's troops deeper into Mexico. When his forces finally took over the capital of Mexico City, Leonor and *La Cruz Blanca* shared in the victory.

Later, Mexico awarded Leonor five medals for her work in 1914. One proclaimed her a veteran of the 1910–1914 campaign. Others honored her for "national merit."

Leonor was a heroine of the war.

After the revolution, Leonor de Magnon settled down to write about her beloved Mexico and her work in *La Cruz Blanca.* She died in 1955, at the age of 79.

Her father's affectionate nickname for Leonor —*La Rebelde*—was truly accurate.

She had been a rebel, as well as a writer, teacher and nurse. It was her independent and adventurous spirit that led her to get involved in dangerous situations, when most people would have sought safety. But her personal courage and daring inspired others to act in the same manner. And the revolutionary effort benefited from her dedication and determination to do what she believed to be right.

Like many young women who had to support their families after World War II, Bette Graham took a job as a secretary. Secretarial jobs provided one of the few careers open to working women. However, the pay was usually low and there was little room for advancement.

Many women substituted for men in higher paying factory and business jobs during World War II. But once the war ended in 1945, veterans came back to fill those jobs. Most married women workers went back home, or took up more traditional "women's jobs." They became sales clerks, school teachers, nurses, telephone operators—and secretaries. These jobs paid less than comparable jobs many men had in factories, businesses, spe-cialized trades or professions.

Many people just assumed that men needed to make more money than women because they were heads of households and had families to support. So people thought it was "natural" for high-paying jobs to go to men and low-paying jobs to women. However, many women were heads of households, too. If a woman were widowed or divorced, or chose to remain unmarried, she had to find a way to support herself—just like a man.

When Bette Graham joined the ranks of more than 63,000 secretaries who worked in Texas in the 1950s, she was the single head of her household, with a young son to support. It was not easy. But Bette was smart and knew that she could do more than type let-ters. Bette was also an artist and inventor. And she developed an office product which helped secretaries all over the world do their jobs more effectively. She called it Liquid Paper, a solution that can be used to paint over typing mistakes. Before Liquid Paper, the only way to correct a typing error was to erase it. Sometimes the erasure tore the paper, or left a messy smudge. No one liked to send out a messy letter or report—especially Bette Graham.

Bette used her talents and imagination to figure out a way to solve the problem of messy typing erasures. In the process, she developed a new product and became a millionaire. And because she cared deeply about others, she gave away much of her wealth. This is Bette Graham's story.

Million-Dollar Inventor
BETTE GRAHAM

(1924–1980)

Bette Nesmith Graham didn't set out to be an inventor or to make a million dollars.

She wanted to be an artist. As a shy, sensitive girl growing up in San Antonio, she developed an eye for color and an appreciation for the way artists captured a scene or an emotion on canvas. So Bette planned a career in art for herself.

However, as it had for many young women and men, World War II interrupted Bette's plans.

Young men all over the United States left their schools, jobs, homes and families to join the armed forces and go off to fight in Europe or Asia. If they were not yet married, many wanted to get married quickly so that someone would be waiting for them when they came home. Bette's high school sweetheart was one of those young men.

Would Bette marry him before he went off to war?

"Yes," Bette said. So she quit school, married and later had a child. Her plans to be an artist would have to wait.

Like thousands of women all over America, Bette waited for her husband to come home from the war. However, many war-time marriages did not survive the difficult strain of the war years, and Bette's was one of these. By the end of the war, Bette was divorced. But now she had a young son, Michael, to support. She had to find a way to earn a living for herself and her child. Studying art was now out of the question.

She moved to Dallas, determined to make a decent life for the two of them. She learned typing and shorthand and got a job as a secretary. Bette was so capable that she soon got a promotion. She served as the executive secretary to a bank president, at a salary of $300 a month.

With her promotion came a brand new electric typewriter. Unlike the old manual typewriters, it had a carbon ribbon that made typing mistakes hard to correct. An erasure just made a messy smudge on the page. Bette was too efficient to spend time retyping letters. So, she looked for a neater way to correct her typing errors.

She had an idea. Artists often painted over their mistakes on canvas. No one ever saw the mistake because the paint covered it.

Bette thought: Why couldn't you paint over a typing mistake? Why couldn't you use a paint to match the paper and hide the mistake so that no one would ever see it? Bette resolved to experiment.

"I decided to use what artists use," Bette said. "I put some tempera waterbase paint in a bottle and took my watercolor brush to the office, and I used that to correct my typing mistakes."

She colored the tempera paint to match the stationery she used. Her boss never noticed!

At first, Bette didn't tell anyone about her new invention. But soon, another secretary noticed Bette correcting her mistakes in this unusual way and asked Bette to give her some of the correcting fluid, too. Bette found a green bottle at home, wrote "Mistake Out" on a label, stuck it on the bottle and gave it to her friend.

Soon she was supplying Mistake Out to all the secretaries in the building.

Other people began to notice as well. An office supply dealer who often visited Bette's building asked her if she'd ever thought about selling her product on a large scale.

"No," Bette said.

But then she did begin to think about it seriously.

Bette had always struggled against mediocrity. She never settled for being "second best" at anything.

"I felt that I was special, that I had something special to give. But I didn't know what that was going to be," she said.

Maybe taking her little product and developing it into a business was something Bette could do well. It might be a way to improve her standard of living. But even more important, it might provide a way for Bette to do something outstanding with her life.

So Bette thought about starting a business. How could she do it?

Bette had no business training, except her secretarial experience. She knew nothing about marketing, distribution, manufacturing or pricing. She had no money to invest. But she did have intelligence and the will to work hard. Most importantly, she believed she could be successful.

Bette decided to take the risk and open her own business.

In 1956, in the kitchen of her North Dallas home, Bette started the Mistake Out Company. (She later renamed her product "Liquid Paper.") Then she filled out the trademark papers herself because she didn't have money to pay an attorney. She couldn't afford to hire a chemist either. So Bette went to the library and found a chemical formula for a type of tempera paint. She got a chemistry teacher from a Dallas high school to help her out. And a man at a paint company showed her how to grind and mix paint. Everything about her new company was "do it yourself." Her first customers were the secretaries she knew.

Bette wanted to convince a national firm to market, advertise and sell Liquid Paper. She made a presentation to International Business Machines Corporation (IBM), the huge computer and office products company. But IBM wasn't interested. They told her to improve her product and come back later.

With this rejection, Bette made an important decision: "I decided to market the product myself. I never did go back to IBM."

Bette had a lot to do in those early days. She had to improve her formula, design the package, develop an advertising campaign and a marketing strategy. She had to find dealers to sell her product and decide how much to charge for it. At the same time, Bette had to keep her full-time secretarial job so she could buy groceries for herself and her son.

But that wasn't all.

"The most difficult challenge was to overcome the fear of failure," she said.

Very few women were active in the world of business. Even fewer had made it big. The chance for success was slim. It might have been easier for a man.

Bette even said she wished she could have turned over a lot of those decisions to a man, ". . . but I didn't have a fellow at that time. So I had to do it myself. I had to . . . appreciate that as a woman, I was strong, complete, adequate."

So she got busy. She recruited new customers by picking companies and office supply dealers from the telephone book.

When Bette got home from her office job at night, she kept working. She turned her kitchen into a laboratory and her garage into a manufacturing plant for a brand new product.

Anyone visiting Bette's North Dallas home might have thought she was crazy.

On her kitchen floor sat paint cans, thinners, brushes, bottles and vats of the finished product. On her countertop sat her home electric mixer which she used to mix her special paint formula.

Her neighbors probably wondered what was going on in the garage as Bette's son Michael and his friends filled tubes and bottles for customers.

Bette probably wondered why she was doing all this, too. After two years of work, she was selling only about 100 bottles a month.

But she didn't give up.

Bette mailed articles about Liquid Paper to magazines read by buyers of office supplies. In October 1958, *The Office* magazine listed Liquid Paper as one of its "new products of the month." That provided the break Bette had been waiting for. Orders began to trickle in every day. Then one afternoon, bone-tired after a full day's work, Bette went to the mail box. One letter caught her eye. It was from General Electric, the famous corporation.

Bette held her breath, opened the letter and read it slowly. The huge company wanted 432 bottles of Liquid Paper!

Bette's heart pounded. Deep down she knew this was the first sign that her company could become something big.

She was right.

"I'll never forget it," Bette said. "General Electric had seen publicity for the product and wanted three gross. I had to work several nights to fill the order but I didn't mind a bit."

Secretaries from some of the biggest companies in America — General Motors, Bethlehem Steel, Owens-Illinois — began ordering tubes or

Gihon Foundation, Dallas

This notice in the October 1958 issue of *The Office* magazine brought in hundreds of orders for Liquid Paper.

bottles of Liquid Paper. They called the product "an answer to a prayer."

One woman added a personal plea to her order: "Will you please send as soon as possible — I feel like a kid who has been promised something. I can hardly wait."

Many of the letters were addressed to "Mr. Nesmith" or "Dear Sir." Bette had signed all the material, "B. Nesmith," believing that people would have more respect for a company with a man as president.

Few of the enthusiastic secretaries ever realized that the business was a one-woman shoestring operation. Bette hesitated to let them know. She wasn't sure whether or not people would buy her product if they knew it was produced in her kitchen!

Bette wrote to one customer, "Our lab is working on a faster-drying solution." As she typed, she knew that her "lab" was her kitchen and she was the only "research assistant."

But the night and weekend work began to take its toll. Frequently Bette would be typing away when she heard a neighbor's rooster crow. Morning had arrived. She had worked all night. Now it was time to get ready for her daytime job!

She wanted to quit her secretarial job. But she feared she couldn't make it with the Liquid Paper business alone. Then one day at work, she made a mistake. Out of habit, she signed her boss's letter with the name of her own little company instead of the name of the firm which employed her. It was a big mistake in the eyes of the boss. He fired Bette!

It was a big shock. Bette still had a son to support, and she needed the steady income from her job. Bette had made very little money selling Liquid Paper, in spite of working nights and weekends. But Bette turned this crisis into an opportunity. With the extra time she had now, she decided to devote full-time to selling Liquid Paper.

Soon, business began to take off. A big San Antonio office supply company placed a large order. A few weeks later, it ordered more. It so surprised Bette that she called to find out if the order was correct.

Sales in office supply stores around the country began to mushroom. The business finally outgrew Bette's kitchen. She bought a portable building and put it in her backyard. It became her laboratory.

One night Bette's date arrived to pick her up and asked, "What's going on in the backyard?" He was Bob Graham. Bette married him in 1962, and Bob became involved in Bette's business. He helped sell the product on the road.

By this time, Bette was selling about 200 to 300 bottles a week, and she hired two college students to fill bottles in her garage. They mixed up five-gallon batches and poured it into ketchup squeeze bottles. Then they filled the tiny Liquid Paper bottles.

By 1963, Bette's workers were filling 500 bottles a week. By 1964, 5,000 bottles a week.

In 1965, Bette moved the whole operation into a four-room house. By 1967, it had grown into a million dollar business. She bought another portable building, and another and another. She joked that she had so many portable buildings that some people thought she had a company that sold portable buildings.

In 1968, Bette Nesmith Graham moved into her own plant and corporate headquarters. She had come a long way from the part-time business in her kitchen. She had fully automated her

Gihon Foundation, Dallas

By 1965, Bette Graham, second from left, had to move her growing business out of her garage into a four-room house, shown here.

Right. When Bette Graham invented Liquid Paper she was a young single mother with a child to support. Her son, Michael Nesmith, helped fill her first orders and later became famous as a member of The Monkees, a popular singing group.
Below. Bette started her business in her kitchen.
Far Right. By 1968, the Liquid Paper Corporation moved into an 11,000 square foot building, and the manufacture of Liquid Paper became a fully automated operation. Bette, at center with shovel, broke ground for the new building.

95

operation. Her workers now operated machines instead of filling bottles by hand. She had 19 employees and that year sold one million bottles.

It had been 10 long years, but she had progressed from selling 100 bottles a month in 1958 to selling 40,000 bottles in one week! She now served as chairman of the board of the new Liquid Paper Corporation.

Bette had always been a very religious person, a follower of Christian Science. As her business grew and the number of employees increased, she was determined to maintain high business ethics. She also placed a high value on the ideas and the personal growth of the individual employees.

The virtues of honesty, unselfishness and wisdom were practical in the business world, she maintained, and what's more they were profitable!

"Yes, I have had the problems of people looking down on my idealism," she told an interviewer. "But all of the time, I have been taking my money to the bank. I have been doing all the

Bette used this ordinary, household mixmaster in her kitchen to mix the paint formula for her first batches of Liquid Paper.

things people said I couldn't do."

In 1968, Bette published a "Statement of Policy" to guide her burgeoning company. It listed many of her beliefs, including one that stated her corporation "acknowledged a relationship with a Supreme Being who uses us as we respond."

Bette's policies continued to pay off. In 1975, Bette presided over the dedication of a new 35,000-square-foot, international headquarters building in Dallas.

Like Bette's home and all her other offices, this huge building was beautiful. She filled the open, airy interior with art and plants. Employees used an on-site library and a child care center.

The plant had equipment that could produce 500 bottles a minute. In 1976, the Liquid Paper Corporation turned out 25 million bottles. Its net earnings were $1.5 million. The company spent $1 million a year on advertising alone.

All this was quite exhilarating for Bette Nesmith Graham. But in 1976, she retired as chairman of the board. She wanted to devote

Reagan Bradshaw, Austin

more time to her religion. And she had a new goal in mind—she planned to establish a philanthropic foundation that would help women develop new roles in society.

In 1976, she set up the Bette Clair McMurray Foundation financed by her royalties from the Liquid Paper invention. She used her money to help women find new ways to earn a living. The foundation has supported, among other programs, a career guidance project for unwed mothers; career counseling, as well as shelter, for battered wives; and college scholarships for older women to use for further training which would upgrade their job status.

In 1978, she established the Gihon Foundation to provide opportunities and resources for women to realize their full potential.

"Most people in my income bracket build estates," she said. "I can't understand why. My estate will be what I can do for others. I want to see my money working, causing progress for people."

She believed money was a tool, not a solution to a problem. The idea for her business came, she pointed out, because she simply tried to solve a problem, not make a lot of money.

Toward the end of her life, Bette Graham was in much demand as a speaker to business and women's groups. In 1977, Bette addressed students at the prestigious Harvard University School of Business. Her business became a successful "case study" for students.

Bette Nesmith Graham died in May 1980. Six months earlier, her Liquid Paper Corporation had been sold for $47.5 million.

She left behind a "handy helper" office product that freed secretaries around the world from a lot of drudgery. She also left behind two private foundations to help women get ahead in business.

But the message she most wanted to leave behind was that love, honesty, beauty and fairness can exist—and flourish—in the business world.

Gihon Foundation, Dallas

The new corporate headquarters of Liquid Paper reflected Bette's concern for artistic design and employee comfort. She planned open, sunlit spaces for her employees and enlivened the walls and hallways with personally selected works of art. She also installed an employee library and child care center.

What did Jane Y. McCallum want more than anything in the world?

Riches? Fame? Adventure? Travel?

No. That's not what Jane wanted.

She just wanted to vote. That's all. She simply wanted to be able to cast her ballot in an election for president of the United States, or for governor of Texas or even for mayor of the city of Austin, where she lived. But Jane and her friends did not have the right to vote for president of the United States. They could not vote—simply because they were women! State and federal laws granted the right to vote to men only!

That made many people angry. They decided to change the laws. People who worked to give women suffrage, the right to vote, were called suffragists.

The struggle for woman's suffrage had been going on in the United States for 50 long, hard years. Jane Y. McCallum and other leaders were able to build on past work and finally achieve success.

Jane Y. McCallum became one of Texas's most effective suffragists. The wife of Austin's school superintendent and the mother of five children, Jane got involved in suffrage through the women's club movement. In the early 1900s, women's clubs started public libraries, organized hospitals, built parks and museums and worked to improve schools. Club work brought many well-educated women out into their communities for the first time. There, they saw children who needed better nutrition and health care. They saw children working in unsafe factories at miserable wages. They saw inadequate schools and horrible prison conditions. And they realized that it would take more than their club work to make their communities better. It would take new laws.

Jane Y. McCallum and thousands of club women like her grew more and more frustrated. They felt that they could not really change things. And they began to ask, "Why not?"

Why couldn't women change laws? Why couldn't they determine how city and school taxes were spent? Why couldn't women vote?

No one ever gave Jane Y. McCallum a good answer. So she joined with other Texas women to win the right to vote. In the process she became a wise and effective political leader. The results of her work caused real changes for Texas. This is Jane Y. McCallum's story.

The Successful Suffragist
JANE Y. McCALLUM

(1878–1957)

Jane Y. McCallum wanted to be a good wife and a good mother to her five children. And she wanted to be a good citizen, too.

Today, mothers can work, have careers or even run for political office if they want to. But in the early 1900s, when Jane was raising her family, she was expected to stay home and manage her large household—and do nothing else!

But Jane Y. McCallum didn't stay home. She dared to enter the world of politics, which at that time was limited to men only!

Why did Jane Y. McCallum become involved in the political world outside her home? Why did a woman with five children take on more work and responsibilities?

"If women aren't interested in politics, they aren't interested in whether their babies get clean milk and whether they use pure cosmetics," Jane said.

Politics meant life, health and safety to Jane. And it also meant having the right to vote.

In the Texas Constitution, women were classified with "children, idiots, lunatics, paupers and felony convicts," who were also denied the right to vote.

This infuriated Jane.

She knew she was smart and she knew a lot about public issues. She got tired of the ridicule and the insults. She saw no sensible reason why women couldn't have a say in public issues.

Jane decided she would use her every spare minute to help women win the right to vote in Texas, and the nation.

It wasn't easy. Although Jane's mother-in-law lived with her and could help with the children, Jane still had to cook, wash and sew for her family. How could she manage? Would she have time to work for suffrage and attend her son Alvaro's football games and track meets? Would she have the time to make her daughter Kathleen's evening dresses and chaperone her parties? Would she have time to help with school homework and bake pies? Would she find the time to entertain and keep the house clean?

Jane decided that she would just have to find the time — somehow. Woman's suffrage was too important to ignore, not just for Jane, but for all of the women in America. So with the help, encouragement and support of her family, Jane began her important work for women.

As a first step, Jane joined the Austin chapter of the Texas Equal Suffrage Association, which by 1914, had 21 local chapters and 2,500 members. New members, like Jane, joined every day as enthusiasm for woman's suffrage spread across the state. They were housewives, librarians, teachers, club members, church leaders and businesswomen. They, too, thought that woman's suffrage was the most important political issue of their time. And they were willing to do whatever was necessary to win the right to vote.

The question was "how?"

How were the members of the Texas Equal Suffrage Association going to win the right to vote for women? The members spent many hours discussing strategy and deciding just what to do.

Basically, these were their options:

1. *Pass an amendment to the United States Constitution and have it approved by the state legislatures.*

2. *Pass an amendment to the Texas Constitution and have it approved by the voters.*

3. *Pass a state law giving women the right to vote in political party primary elections. (The Dem-*

Jane's oldest children, Kathleen and Alvaro.

ocrats and Republicans nominate their candidates in primary elections.)

At one time or another Texas suffragists tried all three options, concentrating their efforts on whichever one had the best chance for success. Passage of the federal amendment to the U.S. Constitution which would give women the right to vote in *all elections* was always a goal. But it was difficult to accomplish. The suffrage amendment had come up before Congress every session for more than 40 years. And it had not passed.

Meanwhile, the Texas suffragists tried to get the vote any way they could. Before Jane's time, Texas suffragists had tried to convince the Texas legislature to pass a state amendment to the Texas Constitution. They had tried in 1895, 1911, and 1913, with no success. But in 1915, when the men of the Texas legislature voted on the state suffrage amendment, it failed to pass by only three votes.

Discouraged? Give up? Never.

Under the leadership of its president, Minnie Fisher Cunningham, the Texas Equal Suffrage

Association prepared for battle in the next session of the Texas Legislature that would meet in 1917. Mrs. Cunningham, Jane and all the other suffragists threw themselves into the massive campaign necessary to convince the men of the Texas Legislature to give women the right to vote. Those were the days before television or radio. Every legislator's vote had to be won through personal contact. That meant that suffrage leaders, like Jane, had to visit personally with individual legislators. They had to write letters. They had to talk to newspaper editors to generate support for their cause. They had to enlist church ministers and educators to help them convince others.

They had to hold lectures and rallies to educate Texans about the suffrage cause. They even had to convince people that votes for women would not harm women — or society! And whatever they did must help convince members of the Texas Legislature to vote for woman's suffrage. It was a big job.

Jane Y. McCallum had always been a good organizer. The suffrage effort put her skills to the most difficult test. Jane had to recruit volunteers, handle the mailings and stage the rallies.

Even more importantly, Jane had to get Texas newspapers to present information about woman's suffrage that would help — not hurt — the cause.

Jane knew that favorable publicity in the newspapers across the state would impress members of the Texas Legislature and help persuade them to vote for woman's suffrage. So Jane organized a statewide publicity effort for the Texas Equal Suffrage Association. She got volunteers lined up to make speeches. She scheduled appointments with newspaper editors. She prepared press releases which listed prominent people who endorsed the suffrage cause. She sent information about suffrage to newspapers on a regular basis. And she even wrote a weekly column for the *Austin Statesman*.

A gifted writer, Jane at first avoided the spotlight and tried to stay behind the scenes. But one night she spent three hours on the telephone trying to line up someone to make a public speech on suffrage. She came up empty-handed.

"I don't see any way out except to take up public speaking," Jane said. So Jane added speechmaking to her suffrage and homemaking duties.

The McCallum household became a beehive of activity. Kathleen, the oldest child, was a student at the University of Texas; four boys were in high school or elementary school. The children and their friends were always dashing in and out.

Jane turned her kitchen pantry into an office. The dining room table usually had so many papers on it that the family had to eat on the screen porch. Jane's bed was covered with notes and letters.

Important visitors arrived at all hours of the day and night to discuss new strategy or to take Jane to committee meetings.

When the children came home from school, they were likely to find their mother on the telephone, campaigning or recruiting workers. Or she might be banging away on the typewriter, pounding out her latest news story or speech.

Often, Jane had to call on members of the Texas Legislature. And some of them were not too friendly to the suffragists.

"Most of us would have preferred facing an army to meeting face to face with a hostile lawmaker," Jane said.

But sometimes it was unavoidable.

One senator, annoyed that he had been called from his work to meet with a woman, listened to Jane for a few minutes and then told her impatiently, "You ought to get married and tend to a woman's business."

"But I am married," she replied.

"Then you ought to be having children."

"I have five. How many do you suggest I have?" Jane said.

"Then you should be home taking care of them."

"They're in school and their grandmother is there in case they get home early."

Flustered, the senator blurted out, "Then you should be home darning stockings!"

It took a lot of courage for women to walk up to legislators and make a pitch for women's rights. Some men still believed women shouldn't even appear at public gatherings, much less stand up and speak for themselves.

It also helped for the women to have a sense of humor.

"Quiet good humor was her hallmark," friends said of Jane. "Scrappy but never strident, both

Above. Jane expertly balanced her active public life with her equally busy family life. She devoted careful and loving attention to her five children as she worked for the future of all children in Texas through her suffrage and legislative reform campaigns. Her children in this 1920s photo were, left to right, Artie, Henry, Kathleen, Alvaro and Brown.

Left. Jane, seated at center rear, and her husband, A. N. McCallum, center front, always presided over holiday dinners, a McCallum family tradition.

Bottom left. Jane, standing third from right, interrupted her busy schedule to go on camping and fishing trips with her family. As her children grew older and married, grandchildren enlarged Jane's close family.

courageous and sweet-natured, she was a vivacious, feminine woman who loved her home and garden, attracted interesting people and did not take herself too seriously."

Because Jane did not take herself too seriously, she was able to brush off insults and personal criticism that might have intimidated others. Once when a legislator implied to her group that "ladylike" women would not *want* to vote, Jane looked him straight in the eye and told him she would not allow his insult to the suffrage workers to go unchallenged.

"You apologize," she demanded, "and do it now."

The startled legislator immediately complied.

Jane said that this exchange was one of the few times she actually got angry in the suffrage effort. She made a practice of controlling her temper; she chose to be effective, not angry.

Jane's children said of her: "Mother believed a person had to *have* a temper to be worth anything, and had to control a temper to *be* anything."

In 1917, the Texas suffragists took on additional duties — "war work." The United States had entered World War I, and the suffragists led the efforts to support the soldiers. They volunteered for the Red Cross, sold Liberty bonds and planted victory gardens.

They believed that their war work would help the suffrage cause. And it did. People began to reason, "Since women are helping win the war, why shouldn't they be able to vote?"

To help with the war effort, Jane headed up a fundraising organization in Austin called the Liberty Loan Committee. And she continued her charity work, her newspaper writing and her lobbying efforts for woman's suffrage. The war years were a hectic time.

"All told, Wednesday, I attended five meetings and cooked three full, good meals," she wrote in her diary June 15, 1917. "Yesterday I sold bonds all day long. Wound up in a Red Cross parade — most blistered."

And the war years were a time for strong emotions. Jane saw her children's friends join the army and go off to France to fight. Her heart ached for them. But when she gave a suffrage speech that was well received, she always got a lift.

103

Small victories also gave her energy. One evening she came home from the Liberty Loan office exhausted. Then she heard the news that President Wilson had endorsed the federal suffrage amendment.

"Did I say tired?" she wrote in her diary. "I never felt better in my life. I feel like I could walk to Washington just to give him a pat."

Although the suffragists did not convince the legislature to pass a state suffrage amendment in the 1917 session, their grass roots political organizing and publicity, as well as the good will generated by their war work, finally began to pay off.

In 1918, the Texas suffragists tried to convince the newly elected governor, William P. Hobby, to support a bill to allow women to vote in the state political party primary elections. When Governor Hobby called a special session and agreed to consider the bill, Jane Y. McCallum and the other suffrage leaders went into action. They were well organized, and they were effective. One leader called them, "the smartest group of politicians in the state."

The suffragists wrote letters, visited, cajoled, persuaded and finally convinced a majority of the members of the legislature to vote for the Primary Election Bill. The Senate passed it 18 to 4.

On March 16, 1918, Jane and her friends sat and waited in the visitors' gallery in the State Capitol building in Austin, while the members of the House of Representatives voted. The Texas House passed the bill 84 to 34. It was a dramatic moment in Texas history.

As the women rose to leave the gallery after the vote, "the men saw us . . . and gave us a perfect ovation, cheering for some minutes . . . It was a surprising and greatly appreciated tribute to the work that the women had been doing," wrote Jane's friend Minnie Fisher Cunningham.

When Governor Hobby signed the Primary Election Bill into law on March 26, among those standing proudly behind him was Jane Y. McCallum. They had finally opened the door!

Texas women could now vote in the upcoming primary elections — only 17 days away. Jane

It was a big day for Jane Y. McCallum when Governor William Hobby signed the Suffrage Proclamation. Jane, third from right on back row, stood behind her friend Minnie Fisher Cunningham.

and her friends mounted a massive effort and helped more than 386,000 women register to vote for the election.

For Jane, it was a triumphant moment. She was 39 years old and wrote in her diary, "Attained my majority at last, thank you, registered to vote. Sixth of Travis County women."

And on election day the women turned out in record numbers for the Democratic primary, nominating Hobby for another term as governor and Annie Webb Blanton for state superintendent of public instruction, both of whom went on to win in the general elections.

But the battle was not over. Voting in a primary election was not *full* suffrage. The general election, in which voters cast ballots for the candidates nominated in the primary elections, was still closed to women. They still couldn't vote in local or special elections.

Texas suffragists were eager to work on passage of the federal amendment; its passage would guarantee, once and for all, that women could vote in *all* elections.

But in 1919, when the Texas Legislature passed a state constitutional amendment and sent it to the voters for approval, the suffragists decided to seize the opportunity. Jane Y. McCallum headed the statewide publicity effort needed to convince the male voters of Texas to pass the amendment. The women couldn't vote—it was not a primary election—but they could campaign for the amendment. And they did.

Jane and other leaders set up campaign training schools for their workers, and they organized the state, precinct by precinct. Jane wrote newspaper articles. She lined up endorsements from World War I soldiers and got ministers to preach Mother's Day sermons in favor of the amendment. She set up suffrage booths in department stores and theater lobbies. She got volunteers to distribute three million leaflets. She got all of Texas's daily newspapers, except one, to endorse suffrage. And she used powerful arguments to make the suffrage point.

When the law giving women the right to vote in Texas party primaries passed, there were only 17 days to register to vote in the upcoming July primary election. The suffragists took to the streets in cars, sporting banners and ringing bells, spreading the news and calling on all Texas women to register.

"If a woman steals from her employer, does her father, husband, brother or son serve out her term in prison? . . . Why is it that the only place in the world a man wants to represent a woman is at the ballot box?" Jane wrote.

It was a close election. The pro-suffrage voters led all through the evening. Women went to bed believing they had won. But the next morning, the results showed them losing by 25,000 votes.

With the door now closed on a state constitutional amendment for suffrage, the women still did not give up.

They went back to work on ratification of the federal suffrage amendment.

Eleven days after the state election, the U.S. Congress passed the federal woman's suffrage amendment and sent it to the state legislatures for ratification. Governor Hobby, by now a strong supporter of woman's suffrage, called the legislature into a special session to vote on the amendment.

Jane and the suffragist leaders had become experts at persuading members of the legislature to take action. This time, it took them only four days to secure a favorable vote. Both the Texas House and Senate ratified the 19th amendment to the United States Constitution on June 28, 1919. Texas was the ninth state in the nation and the first in the South to ratify.

The woman's suffrage amendment (the 19th Amendment) formally became a part of the United States Constitution early the next year. It read: *The right of citizens of the United States to vote shall not be denied by the United States or by any state on account of sex.* Women could now vote in *all* elections.

Jane McCallum was euphoric.

"With high hopes and enthusiasm women stepped forth into a world in which they were citizens at last!" she wrote.

With the vote won at last, Jane could now affect those public issues she cared so deeply about. Her suffrage experiences had made her a seasoned professional in the world of politics. She knew how to pick and win her political battles. And winning began to come more frequently.

More than 386,000 Texas women, including these Travis County suffragists, eagerly registered to vote for the first time in 1918.

During the 1920s, Jane headed up the Joint Legislative Council, a coalition of women's organizations that pushed for reforms in state laws. The press jokingly called Jane's group the "Petticoat Lobby."

"Some women thought that an insult, but I didn't," Jane said. "I thought we should dignify the term."

And that's just what Jane did. The Petticoat Lobby may have been the most successful public interest lobby group in Texas history. It got its entire legislative program passed into laws in the 1920s. The women were responsible for reform of the state's public school system, child labor laws, infant and maternal health programs, the first child welfare programs, prison reforms and a host of other progressive legislation.

By 1926, the power of Jane Y. McCallum and the Petticoat Lobby was so well established that political candidates actively sought their support. The women supported Dan Moody for governor, after he had endorsed their entire legislative program. Moody won the election and appointed Jane Secretary of State in 1927. She became the second woman in Texas history to hold that job, and when Governor Ross Sterling reappointed her to the post in 1931, she became the only person in Texas history to be appointed to the post by two governors.

The suffrage movement and the great legislative lobbying effort had given women like Jane new political experiences and skills. The world of politics was now no longer exclusively for men. Hundreds of Texas women ran for and won political office. By 1929, 109 of the state's 254 county treasurers were women. Women served in the Texas House and Senate. They served on school boards, city councils and county boards. Texans

Secretary of State Jane Y. McCallum presided over the opening of the 1933 Texas Legislature. Governor Dan Moody first appointed her in 1927, and Governor Ross Sterling reappointed her in 1931. Jane was the only Texas Secretary of State to serve under two governors.

even elected a woman governor—Miriam A. Ferguson in 1925 and 1933.

It was not just elective office that women occupied. They were appointed in increasing numbers to public boards and commissions. And in 1925 a session of Texas's highest judicial body was presided over by the "All Woman Supreme Court."

This all happened—for the first time in Texas —because Jane Y. McCallum and women like her decided to leave their safe homes and enter the world of politics.

Jane Y. McCallum may have been one of America's first "superwomen." She did it all. Jane raised five children and, with her husband, enjoyed a rich family life. She developed a career in politics and government. And she helped lead the successful movement which extended the vote to half the citizens of Texas—the women.

Betty Jane McCallum, Austin

Jane Y. McCallum proved that a woman could be a good wife and mother, as well as an outstanding politician and officeholder.

During the suffrage campaign, Jane was so busy she hardly had time to catch her breath. Here's a summary of one day in the life of the McCallum household as recorded in Jane's diary:

May 4, 1918

- *Rose at 5:30 to get Kathleen and Mary Lee (Kathleen's friend) off to Lampasas to appear before School Board.*
- *Cooked their breakfast and served it to them.*
- *Took Mamma's breakfast upstairs as she is not very well.*
- *Finished cooking for rest of family.*
- *Put up a lunch for Alvaro (her oldest son).*
- *Found bushel basket to put potatoes in.*
- *Wrote an hour on my newspaper stuff.*
- *Got children off to school, sending work to Statesman by Arthur. (Had answered three phone calls at intervals.)*
- *Telephoned six people in response to request from Miss Jennie Burleson to get help at her booth.*
- *Cut out curtains for boys' room.*
- *Wrote a lot more for newspaper. (One phone call after another.)*
- *Next door neighbor came in for about 20 minutes.*
- *Ordered groceries and meat and planned a conditional supper (for) two boys, Robert Harris and Skinner Bell to be here if come to track meet.*
- *Ate lunch.*
- *Soaked my useless feet while telephoning about war work.*
- *Mrs. Daniels called in car, took me to Statesman, from where I went to Liberty Loan Headquarters at 2:35.*
- *Worked all afternoon obtaining small subscriptions for $250 pledge for state suffrage.*
- *Forgot to meet with Mrs. Preston's Committee at 3:30 as we were so deep in above.*
- *Got home pretty tired as had gone to bed at 12 the night before.*
- *Mr. and Mrs. J. A. Jackson came in after supper but seeing I had to go out took me to Liberty Loan headquarters.*
- *Phone call awaited me from Mrs. Jackson about how necessary she felt it was for me to go to Burnet today. So to bed at 11 o'clock.*

The signs in Houston said "For Whites Only."

They were posted at the entrances to restaurants, at the airport, over public water fountains, neighborhood swimming pools, the public library—even at City Hall.

Black people were prohibited by law from using the same public facilities as white people in Houston and all over the South. And Christia Adair didn't like it one bit. It was unfair, she thought. It was an injustice. In fact, Christia believed that those "whites only" signs and the laws which allowed them violated the United States Constitution. And like other blacks all over the country, Christia began to challenge those laws. As executive secretary of the Houston chapter of the National Association for the Advancement of Colored People (NAACP) in the 1940s and 1950s, Christia took on the mayor of Houston, Harris County officials and even state officials. And Christia won. Her persistence and belief in the equality of all Americans —black and white—led her to victory after victory.

This is her story.

Civil Rights Crusader
CHRISTIA ADAIR
(b. 1893)

Christia Daniels Adair was born in 1893 and grew up in the little town of Edna, Texas. It was there that her father, Handy Daniels, hauled everything from cotton to crude oil to pianos for local residents. But Handy Daniels loved politics, and he expected Christia and her brothers and sisters to sit at the family table every evening for a discussion about current political events. And Christia didn't much like it.

"It was boring," she said. But Christia learned that participating in the political discussion was a family responsibility and that her father expected her to take a knowledgeable, active role in the family discussions.

Christia's mother expected even more of her. Ada Daniels was very active in her church, and she wanted her children to help whenever they were called on. So Christia had to work at church suppers and help with Sunday school meetings. She recognized her duty to assume church responsibility— and even to become a leader among the group.

"My parents set a standard I had to stretch to reach," Christia said.

This standard included education. Although Christia's parents had not attended school, they expected their children to get a good education. When Christia was about 16, they sent her to high school in Austin. And in 1914, Christia became a student at the all-black state college, Prairie View State Normal and Industrial College (now known as Prairie View A&M).

After Christia finished college, she taught at her old elementary school in Edna. But her father encouraged her to take a job in the nearby town of Vanderbilt so she could earn more money—$40 a month.

Christia took her father's advice and moved to Vanderbilt. And she was glad she did. Because it was there that she met handsome Elbert Adair, a brakeman for the Missouri and Pacific Railroad. They married in May, 1918, and moved to Kingsville in South Texas.

Kingsville surprised Christia. On the edge of the huge King Ranch and only a few miles from the Texas Gulf Coast, it was a dusty, flat railroad town. It had become a center for hauling cattle to market and a shopping area for the large ranches of South Texas. The town's 7,000 residents lived in separate, segregated neighborhoods for blacks, whites and Mexican-Americans. The church in the black section of Kingsville didn't even have a Sunday school. And there were few social or cultural activities that a young, educated black woman could attend. Because Elbert didn't want his wife to work at a job outside their home, Christia had little to do. But she had too much energy to sit at home. Christia found volunteer work.

First, she organized a Sunday school for the children in the black church. Then she got Kingsville's black and white women's clubs to work together to shut down an illegal gambling house on the edge of town.

Because the women succeeded in that goal, they took on another joint effort. This time, they worked together in the campaign to win the right to vote for women. In Kingsville, the white women's clubs were urging people to sign their names to petitions in order to demonstrate widespread public support for votes for women. Christia and many of the other black women in Kingsville helped them.

Texas women won the right to vote in the state party primary elections in 1918. Christia and her friends were delighted. They were eager to cast their first ballots.

"We dressed up and went to vote," Christia said.

But when she and her friends got to the primary election polling place, they were turned away. Election officials would not let them vote.

Christia was puzzled. She asked, "Why can't we vote?"

The election officials offered only vague answers.

"They gave us all different kinds of excuses . . . but we just stayed," Christia said.

Finally, one of Christia's friends asked the officials, "Are you saying that we can't vote because we're black?"

"Yes," the official said. "Blacks don't vote in the political party primary election in Texas."

Christia was dismayed. She couldn't vote because she was black!

"That just hurt our hearts real bad, and we went on. There was nothing we could do about that but just take it as it was," she said.

But Christia remembered this incident, and how much it hurt her.

Another incident in Kingsville hurt Christia's feelings as well.

Republican presidential candidate Warren G. Harding was touring Texas on his 1920 campaign and planned to stop in Kingsville.

Because Christia's husband worked for the railroad, he knew exactly when Harding's train would arrive and where it would stop. He told Christia so that she could arrive early enough to see the man who might become president of the United States.

Christia was thrilled. Warren G. Harding was one of the most famous people ever to come to Kingsville. Christia thought that some of the black school children should go to see him on this special occasion, too, and she took some members of her Sunday school class to the train station. She lined up the children on the platform, exactly where the train would stop with Mr. Harding.

The children waited excitedly. First they heard the train whistle in the distance. They saw the steam locomotive pull into the station. Finally the huge wheels of the train screeched to a halt in front of the platform. The door opened. And there was Warren G. Harding standing right in front of them.

Christia's Sunday school children began calling his name and extending their hands to greet him.

But to their great surprise—and dismay—Warren G. Harding didn't even look at them. Instead, he reached over their heads and shook hands with a group of white children.

Christia was stunned.

Discrimination against blacks had always been a part of her life. She was used to it. After all, she had always lived in the South where some people still retained bitter memories of the Civil War. But in her wildest nightmares, Christia had never believed that a candidate for president of the United States would discriminate against little black children!

"I pulled my children out, hurt, disappointed, and sorry for the children," Christia said.

But she could not forget the incident and vowed to herself to do something to see that all blacks would be treated fairly.

Several years later in Houston, she got the opportunity to keep that vow.

Elbert Adair's job took him to Houston in 1925. He and Christia joined the Methodist Church there. Christia became very active in church work and offered her services as a volunteer to the National Association for the Advancement of Colored People (NAACP).

The NAACP had organized nationally to fight discrimination against blacks by challenging laws that were unfair and perhaps unconstitutional. It was also involved in seeing that existing laws protected blacks as well as whites. Occasionally, blacks who were accused of crimes were beaten or even killed by unruly mobs before they received their constitutional guarantee of a fair trial. The NAACP began to provide lawyers and other assistance to blacks who were charged with crimes.

Many church workers became NAACP volunteers. Like Christia, they were outraged at the injustices they now saw.

Although Christia had seen—and been the victim of—discrimination before, she had experienced nothing like what she saw in Houston. One case near Houston particularly upset her. A black man was accused of a crime. An NAACP lawyer defended him at his trial. The jury found the man "not guilty." But as he was leaving the courthouse, someone shot and killed him anyway.

This incident so disturbed Christia that she made a very important decision about her future: the NAACP would become her life work.

She increased her volunteer hours and became more and more involved with the organization. When Elbert died in 1943, Christia began to spend all of her time working for the NAACP.

The NAACP filed one lawsuit against dis-

crimination that was very close to her heart. A Houston dentist had tried to vote in the state's Democratic primary election and had not been allowed to because he was black. The NAACP brought suit against the State of Texas on his behalf, and the case went all the way to the United States Supreme Court. The NAACP won the lawsuit in 1944. Blacks could vote at last in the political party elections, as well as the November general elections. Nearly 30 years after she had worked for woman's suffrage in Kingsville, Christia Adair finally was allowed to vote in a state primary election. Christia experienced a sweet victory.

But the NAACP did not have many victories in the 1940s. Christia became executive secretary of the Houston NAACP chapter when it was very unpopular to do so. Many people in the South objected to changing the ways blacks were

Courtesy of Willie L. Gay, Houston

Right. Christia Adair, second from right on front row, attended a racially segregated school in Edna.

Below. Because Christia's parents valued a good education, they sent her to Huston College in Austin to complete high school. Christia is shown at the far left.

Courtesy of the Houston Public Library, Houston Metropolitan Research Center

In 1918 Christia married Elbert Adair, a brakeman for the Missouri and Pacific Railroad. Elbert's railroad jobs took the couple first to Kingsville, then to Houston.

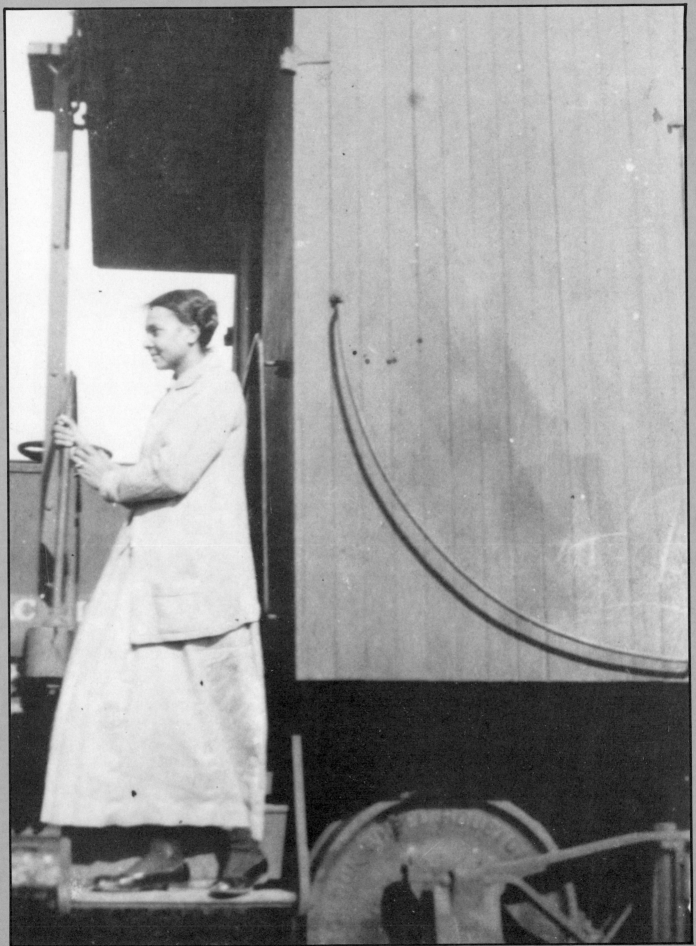

treated. Some hated the NAACP for its efforts to improve the legal and political situation of Texas's black residents. It was hard to raise the money to finance the NAACP's legal activities. Christia fought an uphill battle just to keep the organization alive.

Sometimes she had to worry about keeping herself alive, too. The NAACP office received so many bomb threats that the building's landlord wanted to evict them. Many nights, Christia feared going home by herself. And often, she didn't sleep, wondering if someone might be lurking outside her window.

Many NAACP members urged her to resign, so that she could feel safe again. But Christia chose to risk her life. She believed her work was too important to stop.

Christia "shrugged off threats, the bad telephone calls, the curses that ignorant people sought to inflict on her. . . . She paid no attention when a lot of women would have panicked," one friend said.

Some friends even urged her to buy a gun to protect herself.

"I never had a gun . . . but they thought I did. I did a lot of big talking," Christia laughed.

Christia continued talking and working all through the 1940s and 1950s. And she, and the NAACP, finally began to achieve some victories. Under her leadership, the NAACP was responsible for these changes in Houston:

- The "whites only" signs came down at the Houston airport. Blacks were finally allowed to sit in the main waiting room, use the restrooms and eat in the restaurant.

- A Houston grand jury, using testimony given by Christia and other NAACP leaders, ordered the police department to stop using "whipping posts" where black prisoners were questioned about crimes and sometimes beaten if they refused to confess.

- Houston county government began to hire blacks for clerical jobs for the first time.

- Blacks could sit anywhere they wanted on Houston buses, instead of at the back of the bus as they had been required to do for decades.

- Blacks won the right to serve on trial juries and grand juries, and thus were able to play a role in Houston's judicial system for the first time.

- Houston newspapers began referring to blacks as "Mr., Mrs. or Miss," just like they did for whites, instead of calling blacks by their first names only.

- The Veterans Hospital began to allow blacks to use the swimming pool and barber shop.

These were, by and large, legal victories. Christia was also interested in seeing that blacks were treated fairly in ordinary transactions of every day life — such as when they went to the grocery store or tried to buy clothes in a department store. One thing in particular bothered Christia.

All her life, Christia had never been able to try on clothes in a department store before she bought them. Many stores just didn't let black men, women or children try on clothes. Those which did often made blacks use separate fitting rooms from whites.

Christia decided it was time to do something about the way most department stores treated blacks.

She walked into a big downtown Houston store, picked out a garment and asked to try it on.

The sales lady hesitated. Then she led Christia back to the alteration room, where clothes were hemmed up or taken in for customers.

"I don't want to try it on in the alteration room," Christia said. "I want to try it on in the fitting room like all the other ladies do."

After confronting the store's manager, who didn't want any bad publicity, Christia got to try on the garment in the fitting room. From that time on, black women were able to try on clothes in Houston shops. And Christia Adair had won one more battle in her fight against discrimination — this time it was the battle of the fitting room!

As the years went by, all of this work began to take its toll on Christia. By 1959, she was 66 years old. She had managed to keep the NAACP alive, even though powerful politicians had tried to run the organization out of the state.

"My brains felt like they were giving way. I

The Houston chapter of the National Organization for Women honored Christia Adair for her efforts to gain the right to vote. She was one of only a few black women active in the Texas suffrage movement.

122

The Houston Chapter
of the
National Organization for Women
and its
Task Force on Minority Women & Women's Rights
wish to honor
Suffragette

Christia Adair

on the
54th Anniversary
of
Women's Suffrage
August 26, 1974

Her life is a history of the struggle of women and minorities in this society.

knew I had reached the end of my capacity and told everyone I would have to retire," she said.

Although Christia stepped down as executive secretary of the NAACP, she didn't stop her work to end discrimination.

She became active in the Democratic party precinct organizations in the 1960s, and she joined in the civil rights demonstrations to open up even more public facilities to blacks. She watched the courts strike down discriminatory local, state and federal laws. And she saw the United States Congress enact the landmark Civil Rights Act of 1964.

Many people began to recognize that Christia Adair's early work for the NAACP had paved

WELCOME TO
HARRIS COUNTY
CHRISTIA V. ADAIR PARK

Harris County Parks System, Houston

In 1977, on her 84th birthday, Harris County named a park in Christia Adair's honor because of her many years of community service.

the way for some of the later victories in the battle against discrimination. In 1977, Harris County named a Houston park after her—on Christia's 84th birthday.

Christia thought segregation of the races was "the cruelest thing that could ever happen to people. Not only to blacks, but to all people, period."

Everyone suffered from segregation, Christia believed.

Christia Adair helped put an end to widespread discrimination in Houston. And she did so in a way that avoided the violence that occurred in other southern cities with similar problems.

"She was always able to conduct herself as a lady with honor and integrity, and she never became discouraged," friends said of her.

As a child, Christia always thought of herself as a person who could do anything she wanted to do. As an adult, Christia did what she believed to be right and honorable.

Her family and church were the starting points.

"That's where I learned to serve," she said.

"That's where I learned to live. That's where I learned if I ever wanted friendship, I must be a friend."

Christia Adair was a true friend for people everywhere who fought against racial discrimination.

Harris County Parks System, Houston

CORNELIA ADAIR

MOLLY GOODNIGHT

Palo Duro Canyon in the Texas Panhandle is one of the great scenic wonders in America—a smaller version of the Grand Canyon. The Palo Duro is 120 miles long and has an elevation of 3,500 feet at the rim. The sheer canyon walls and steep gorges were formed by water erosion more than 90 million years ago. The canyon provides a protected shelter from the fierce northerly winds of the plains, and its abundant water and grasses have made it a haven for wild animals.

Spaniard Francisco Vasquez de Coronado was the first European to visit the canyon, probably around 1541. It was hundreds of years before others followed him. Because the canyon offered such natural protection, the Palo Duro was one of the last American Indian strongholds on the plains. Anglo-Americans did not begin to settle the area until after General Ranald S. MacKenzie defeated a large force of Indians in the canyon in 1874.

Famed cattleman Charlie Goodnight was the first to see the potential of the canyon for cattle grazing, and with the financial backing of English-man John Adair and his wife Cornelia, he drove the first herd of 1,800 cattle into the canyon to set up a 25,000 acre ranch in 1876. Goodnight's wife, Molly, established the first home in the Panhandle there in 1877.

The cattle business in America was very profitable in the 1870s, but it required a great deal of money. Few Americans, particularly the cowboys in the West who understood the business, had enough money to buy a herd and grazing land, or to ship the cattle to market. Wealthy Europeans, like John and Cornelia Adair who were looking for profitable American investments, financed many western cattle operations. The Goodnight-Adair partnership turned out to be most profitable for them—and for the entire Texas Panhandle. They named their spread the JA Ranch, for John Adair's initials. By 1885, it had 1.3 million acres and more than 100,000 head of cattle. It encompassed parts of six Panhandle counties, making it one of the largest and most successful ranches in America.

Building a ranch this size would be difficult anywhere in the world. But it was particularly hard on the high plains of Northwest Texas. High winds, alternating bitter cold and extreme heat, the sheer barrenness of the landscape and the lack of water, made settlement in the Panhandle difficult. Ranches were often hundreds of miles apart. Neighbors might see each other only once a year. The loneliness was particularly hard on the wives. Many of these women left their parents, friends and relatives to start ranches in the distant West with their husbands and children.

Yet hundreds of pioneer women, like Cornelia Adair and Molly Goodnight, managed to survive the hardship and loneliness of life on the high plains. And they not only survived, they thrived—with spirit and hope intact! They endured because they believed in what they were doing—settling a new land. Cornelia Adair and Molly Goodnight sacrificed the comforts of easier lives elsewhere to make their dreams come true in the Palo Duro Canyon. In so doing, they shaped the history of the canyon, and the entire Texas Panhandle. This is their story.

The Women of the JA Ranch

CORNELIA ADAIR

(1838–1921)

MOLLY GOODNIGHT

(1839–1926)

Cornelia Adair spurred her horse across the empty plains.

Molly Goodnight followed close behind, struggling to keep her wagon steady over the bumpy grassland.

Together with their husbands — famed cattleman Charlie Goodnight and the wealthy Englishman John Adair — they were driving cattle into the dreaded "Staked Plains" of the Texas Panhandle. It was a haven for outlaws and a hunting ground of the Comanche Indians.

Why would Cornelia, a wealthy and aristocratic woman, ride a horse on this bleak 400-mile journey from Colorado?

Why would school teacher Mary Ann "Molly" Goodnight drive the jolting supply wagon that great distance?

Why would these two civilized women leave comfortable homes and good lives to travel across this barren prairie? How could they endure the forbidding scenes they saw day after day? No trees, shrubs or hills. No trading posts, no ranches, no water. No signs of human life to break the monotonous landscape.

They must have wondered at times themselves. It must have been hard to remember the reasons why they had started out on this grim journey.

But they had a goal. They shared with their husbands the dream of starting a cattle ranch in the untamed, unpopulated Palo Duro Canyon.

The Canyon! Oh, what stories they had heard about it. Charlie Goodnight had seen it and told them about the wild grasses that would feed thousands of head of cattle. He told them about the river — the Prairie Dog Town Fork of the great Red River — and how it had cut fantastic gorges from the canyon's sheer red rock walls. He told them about the cottonwood, wild chinaberry, hackberry and cedar trees that provided lush greenery and cool shade. He told them about the wild colors at sunset whose rare beauty would bring tears to their eyes. Those stories — and the dream of building the finest cattle empire in the West — made them want to go to Palo Duro Canyon more than anything else in the world!

But the trip over the hot treeless plains was beginning to weaken the enthusiasm of the two women. They were tired and dirty. Their backs ached from the strain of riding every day. They worried about the Indians who still roamed the area looking for the ever-dwindling herds of buffalo.

Their patience was wearing thin. And then there was real trouble.

Ten days into the trip, the bone-weary group ran out of water. The cattle and horses were in danger of dying. Had they wandered off the trail? What had gone wrong? Where was the canyon? Everyone felt lost in an endless sea of prairie grass.

Molly's husband, Charlie, set out to find water. No sooner was he out of sight than Molly thought she spotted a band of Indians approaching. The group huddled in fear the entire day, waiting for an Indian attack.

To their relief, it never came. Instead, Charlie Goodnight reappeared that evening with a joyful whoop. He had found water—and the canyon!

The next morning, Molly and Cornelia and the rest of their group followed Charlie to a break in the prairie. At last, they stood on the rim of the great Palo Duro Canyon! What Molly and Cornelia saw took their breaths away.

The canyon was deep and wide. The setting sun cast orange and purple shadows on the steep walls. A golden haze hung over the meandering river at the floor of the canyon. Green plants grew out of the copper soil. And even more wondrous, a thousand buffalo grazed silently on the banks of the river.

The Palo Duro Canyon was everything they hoped it would be.

Cornelia Adair and Molly Goodnight embraced each other in delight and wonder. They kissed their husbands. They cried tears of happiness. They were the first non-Indian women to see the breath-taking Palo Duro Canyon. They rested with their joy for a while on the rim of the canyon. And then they went to work.

They still had to clear a road to get the wagons and all of their supplies down into the canyon. It took two days to build the four-mile road. One night the Adairs and Goodnights got caught in a terrible storm, which made the buffalo herd in the canyon as nervous as the travelers.

"The downpour was terrific," Charlie Goodnight said. "And the lightning a blaze of light, intense, with thousands of flashes on the wagonsheet."

But it was the sound of the restless buffalo that worried Molly and Cornelia.

"The volume from the sound of a herd of buffalo is great . . . with numerous stampedes making it appear to be very close. The night that followed I shall never forget," Charlie Goodnight said. But the storm—and the rampaging buffalo—spared the Goodnights and the Adairs. Dawn brought relief.

When the group finally reached the floor of the canyon, they found the two-room cabin Goodnight had built for them on his earlier trip. At last they could put the rigors of their journey behind them.

The Palo Duro Canyon was now home. First, they spent two weeks exploring its wonders. Then they started to build their new life—and a great cattle empire.

CORNELIA ADAIR

It was Cornelia Adair who turned her husband's vision westward, enabling them to embark on the JA Ranch venture with the Goodnights.

This aristocratic young woman, who was born in New York, fell in love with the American West.

As a young girl in a privileged family, she read stories about the wild animals, the prairies, the Indians and the adventures of the West. Once grown, she longed to see the West herself. But the American Civil War intervened. Cornelia's first husband, Montgomery Ritchie, died of an illness resulting from his Civil War service.

Cornelia, now a widow with a small child, married wealthy Englishman John Adair in 1869, and he took her to live in England on one of his vast estates. But Cornelia couldn't forget her dreams about the "Wild West." In 1874, Cornelia talked him into taking a hunting trip in the American West.

In those days, it was quite fashionable for Easterners and Europeans to take a train out West and hunt buffalo, antelope and other wild game. They considered it a great sport, much like a safari into Africa, and they loved to see first hand what others only read about in stories of the Indians and life in the West.

The Adairs launched their adventure on a Mississippi River steamboat. As they coursed down the river, through the middle of the continent, Cornelia grew spellbound. She wrote in her diary: "Why attempt to describe it? Only poets should write of such scenes of enchantment."

She watched an eagle soar over the bluffs to the prairies west of the river.

"How I longed to follow his example," she wrote, "only to have one glimpse of the prairie which stretches away from the summit of the bluffs—the prairie that I had read of and heard described a thousand times, but never seen."

They left the river, headed west and finally began their buffalo hunt in western Nebraska.

The first night around the campfire, their guides entertained the Easterners with wartime and hunting stories. Later in her wagon, Cornelia, the only woman in the party, couldn't sleep. She had a vague sense of fear as she listened to the shrill cry of the coyote, but it added to her excitement. She peered out of her wagon just before dawn to see Indian guides standing guard by their ponies. Cornelia was thrilled. She was finally in the middle of a scene from the Wild West.

The next day, the hunting party visited a Sioux Indian settlement and because so few white women were in that part of the country, Cornelia became the object of great curiosity.

"It was like a dream, it seems too strange to be true," she wrote. The painted faces of some of the Indians frightened her somewhat, but the beadwork, mother-of-pearl necklaces and earrings "made me quite envious," she continued.

After a meal of meat, beans and coffee, Cornelia's hunting party leaders asked the Indians for advice on the best way to kill buffalo. There was cold silence, then angry words. The Sioux were furious. They wanted the white hunters to stop killing buffalo. Buffalo meat provided food for their people, and the buffalo were becoming scarce. The Sioux believed the hunting party only wanted buffalo for the skins or sport, a waste of the buffalo that threatened the survival of the Indians in the West. Cornelia and her companions left quickly. They did not want to anger the Sioux any more with their talk of hunting buffalo.

Actually, Cornelia and her hunting companions killed only one buffalo the entire trip. They saw few herds and when they did, they could hardly get close enough for a kill.

But it was not just the hunt that fascinated Cornelia. It was the land itself.

"Even when we rode, as we sometimes did for hours almost quite silently, there was something exhilarating in the air, in the wonderful sense of freedom, with the vast open expanse in every direction," she wrote.

The hunting adventure convinced the Adairs to move their American investment business from New York to Denver. John began searching for a way to get into the cattle business. Cornelia relished the chance to have some permanent tie to the West.

In Denver, everyone told John that there was only one man who knew the cattle business inside-out. That man was Charlie Goodnight.

John Adair sought out Charlie, and the two men liked each other immediately. Charlie had big dreams for a huge cattle empire in a little-known canyon in the Panhandle of Texas. But his dreams required money, and not many American cattlemen had as much money as Charlie needed. John Adair did. And more importantly, John Adair was excited about the prospect of becoming an American cattle baron. So John and Charlie entered into a partnership, and Charlie proposed a visit to his fledgling ranch in the Palo Duro Canyon in the Texas Panhandle.

Cornelia was not about to be left alone in Denver! She would go to the Palo Duro, too. She looked foward to traveling with the Goodnights.

The partnership of the Adairs and the Goodnights began. And it created one of the most successful American ranches in history.

MARY ANN "MOLLY" GOODNIGHT

Her name was Mary Ann Dyer, but everybody called her Molly. So Molly it was.

Her mother died when she was only 16, and since Molly was the oldest child in the family—and a girl—it became her responsibility to raise her younger brothers. She became a substitute mother to her family, taking care of the cooking, washing, mending and all of the domestic chores. Then when her father died, she had to take on the money-making chore for the family, as well. She supported herself and the family by teaching school in Weatherford, Texas. Then she met Charlie Goodnight.

Goodnight was an Indian scout and rancher who began driving cattle to markets in New Mexico in 1865. The Goodnight-Loving Trail, one of the most widely used cattle trails in the Southwest, was named for him and his partner, Oliver Loving. A Civil War veteran, Colonel Charlie Goodnight was dashing and adventurous when Molly met him. He was already famous as one of the most successful cattlemen in the West. Charlie and Molly married in 1870 and went to Colorado where Charlie set up a ranch. The ranch venture was not as successful as he had hoped, so he picked out a site for a new ranch in 1876. This time it would be in the isolated Palo Duro Canyon.

Charlie's partner in the new ranch was Englishman John Adair who was eager to invest his money in the prosperous American cattle business. It was an ideal partnership. John had the money and Charlie had the cattle experience.

Molly was in California visiting relatives when Charlie established his partnership with Adair and went to the Palo Duro Canyon to start up the JA Ranch. But she was impatient to rejoin Charlie and insisted that he meet her in Denver so that they could have a proper home.

"Either leave the Panhandle and come out to civilization or I will go to the ranch in Palo Duro," she wrote Charlie.

Charlie hurried to finish a small cabin in the canyon and rushed back to Denver to meet

Molly. He promised to take her to Palo Duro. John and Cornelia Adair were eager to see the Palo Duro Canyon, too. So Charlie escorted Molly, the Adairs and 1,800 head of cattle into the canyon in 1877.

Molly and Cornelia were the first women to make such a trip. Then Cornelia returned to her home in Denver, and it was Molly who established the first permanent home in the Panhandle. Many people believe that the JA Ranch would not have survived the first winter of 1877–1878 if it had not been for Molly Goodnight.

Molly turned her rough little cabin into a real home, and she made the desolate ranch headquarters into a civilized community. Charlie correctly thought the Palo Duro Canyon would be an ideal place for cattle. Molly set out to prove that people could survive as well as those prized cattle.

The only other people on the ranch that first winter were the cowboys who tended the herds. Molly helped the lonely cowboys feel at home on the isolated ranch. She patched their clothes, sewed on their buttons, nursed them when they were ill, wrote letters to their mothers or sweethearts and listened to their troubles when they

were sad. Every day, she rode out to the far reaches of the ranch and visited with the cowboys who were in charge of rounding up stray cattle and looking out for outlaws or Indians.

Molly even set up a Sunday School for the cowboys. She taught them to read, lent them her Bible and brought books for them to share.

On holidays, Molly cooked festive dinners and held parties to cheer up the cowboys who might be thousands of miles from their homes and relatives. She provided love, comfort and gaiety on those special occasions when lonely cowboys, often no more than 16 years old, might especially miss home. The cowboys affectionately began calling her "Aunt Molly."

Even while Molly helped the cowboys overcome the isolation of ranch life, she was trying to fight off her own overwhelming loneliness. After Cornelia Adair's departure. Molly was the only Anglo woman in the Panhandle. She lived 200 miles from the nearest settlement. She had no women friends to talk with and no contact with the world beyond the JA cowboys and the cattle.

The weather, particularly the constant wind, and the threat of Indian attacks made Molly feel especially isolated and vulnerable.

"If there had been no outside dangers, the loneliness would not have been so bad," she said. Molly longed for companionship. Charlie was often away, and Molly spent her days—even weeks—alone in her little cabin.

One day, an adoring cowboy came by with a gift of three chickens for Molly's Sunday dinner. Instead of cooking them, she kept them as pets. The new companions relieved her loneliness.

"No one could ever know what a pleasure those chickens were to me and how much company they were," she said. "They were something I could talk to, they would run to me when I called them, and follow me everywhere I went. They knew me and tried to talk to me in their language."

The example of the JA led other families into the area. Molly soon learned that 75 miles to the north another woman, Molly Bugbee, was starting the Quarter Circle T Ranch with her husband. Although she saw her new neighbor only every six months or so, the knowledge that another woman lived out there on the plains gave Molly a lift.

Years later, when the JA was a well-established institution, the JA cowboys saved their money and bought Molly a silver service to show their appreciation. And her husband gave her a tall clock inscribed:

In Honor of
Mrs. Mary Dyer Goodnight
Pioneer of the Texas Panhandle
For many months in 1877–78, she saw few men and no women, her nearest neighbor being seventy-five miles distant, and the nearest settlement two hundred miles. She met isolation and hardships with a cheerful heart and danger with undaunted courage. With unfailing optimism, she took life's varied gifts and made her home a house of joy.

THE JA RANCH AND THE PANHANDLE

After the first few rough years, the JA Ranch prospered in a big way. By 1882, Charlie was able to buy an additional 93,000 acres to add to his original 25,000. After only five years of operation, the ranch showed a clear profit of $512,000.

The JA grew into a huge community. The Ranch had 50 houses for its cowboys and their families, as well as for new settlers now pouring into the Panhandle. Charlie and his men built hundreds of miles of roads, 30 water tanks, 25 corrals, hundreds of miles of fences and a hay farm.

When Molly finally got some help with her daily domestic chores, she was free to take a more active part in the management of the JA. She had Charlie design a sidesaddle especially for her so she could ride with him out on the range. Molly frequently handled the business transactions of the Ranch, reviewing the accounts and checking the contracts for cattle sales. And she continued to serve as hostess for the ranch community.

Over the years, John and Cornelia Adair visited the JA frequently, and Molly and Cornelia had a chance to continue the friendship they started on that first trip to Palo Duro Canyon in 1877.

By 1885, the JA had 1.3 million acres and 100,000 head of cattle. Its success was assured. But the operation—and the Panhandle—were changing.

John Adair died in 1885. As his widow, Cornelia became Goodnight's full partner in the JA Ranch. She took a strong interest in the management of the Ranch and became even more active in the cattle business than her husband John had been.

By 1887, Molly and Charlie Goodnight were ready to move on to something else. They had

Above. The JA Ranch headquarters in the mid-1880s.

Right. Cornelia Adair and Charlie Goodnight in 1917, long after Cornelia became the sole owner of the JA Ranch.

134

met their challenge on the JA Ranch—and they had made a fortune in the cattle business. They sold their interest in the JA to Cornelia and said good-bye to the Palo Duro Canyon.

Molly and Charlie settled to the east of the canyon and founded the Panhandle town of Goodnight.

Thus, Cornelia became the sole owner of the JA Ranch. She was one of the few women in the world to preside over such a huge business and financial empire. And she loved every minute of it! She visited the JA each fall and rode the range with the cowboys. She presided over the business, hiring and firing managers and authorizing purchases and sales.

The success of the JA spurred development of the entire Texas Panhandle. Small towns began to spring up everywhere. The railroad was built in 1887, making cattle shipment to markets easier. The settlement which later became Amarillo was established that same year, and by 1890, Amarillo was one of the largest cattle shipping points in the world. The city grew rapidly. Merchants arrived. Settlers built schools, churches and homes in the

area, where only prairie grass had grown before. The entire Panhandle underwent swift change. The open range was ending. Smaller ranches were established. Farmers settled in the area.

Cornelia realized that the change would affect the JA. She sensed that the days of huge cattle operations might be limited. And she began to sell some of her vast ranch lands to the newcomers. But Cornelia made a point of meeting the families who bought JA land. She entertained them at the ranch headquarters and at the home she built for herself at nearby Clarendon.

Cornelia became deeply involved in the development of a more civilized life for the Panhandle. She built a hospital and Clarendon's first YWCA, which was later converted into the City Hall. She also supported the building of the first Episcopal Church in the Panhandle.

Although Cornelia Adair grew up amid lavish wealth in New York, she loved the rugged Panhandle plains and western life. During her annual fall visits to the JA Ranch, Cornelia, seated at far left, rode with the cowboys and shared in their chuckwagon meals on the range.

Courtesy of the Panhandle-Plains Historical Museum, Canyon

Meanwhile in their new home at Goodnight, Charlie and Molly also contributed to the changing pattern of life in the Panhandle. They established two churches near Goodnight. But their main concern was to develop educational opportunities for young people in the Panhandle. In 1900, they put up $30,000 to establish their own college, Goodnight College. They provided scholarships for students and let many live in their home.

The Goodnights also maintained the only domestic buffalo herd in the country. Molly, who had been frightened by the stampeding buffalo she encountered in the storm in the Palo Duro Canyon in 1877, became their savior. She was horrified by the relentless slaughter of the animals for sport, and by cattlemen who killed the buffalo to make more grazing room for cattle. But the buffalo hunters didn't kill the young buffalo calves. They left them to starve on the range. Molly decided to try to save those calves herself. She took in four little buffalo calves, raised them on a bottle and started a domestic herd.

The herd prospered and by 1920, Molly had more than 200 buffalo on her ranch in Goodnight. The proceeds from her sale of buffalo helped finance the building of Goodnight College.

Both Molly Goodnight and Cornelia Adair grew to maturity with the Texas Panhandle. The two women nurtured their dreams, and they prospered, along with the Panhandle. Molly Goodnight made her pioneer home. Cornelia Adair had her western adventure. In the process, they helped launch one of the world's most famous cattle empires. And they influenced the history of the Texas Panhandle.

Cornelia Adair died in 1921, and Molly Goodnight, in 1926. But the JA Ranch lives on. It remains a strong presence in the Panhandle today, and it is run by Cornelia's heirs.

Below. **In 1900 Molly and Charlie established Goodnight College, shown here.**

Right. **Even in her old age, Molly Goodnight remained a determined pioneer. She started the first domestic buffalo herd in the country.**

Women Airforce Service Pilots, WWII

Walt Disney Studios created this cartoon symbol, "Fifinella," for the Women's Airforce Service Pilots.

World War II was a difficult time for America. But it was also a time of patriotic fervor, when men and women wanted to help their country face its greatest military danger.

Millions of American soldiers fought in Europe and Asia. They waged battles on land, sea and air. They took risks. They showed courage and bravery daily. Often they had to obey orders which placed them in great danger. Thousands lost their lives.

One group of military pilots had a very unusual assignment during World War II. They never took part in combat operations. Instead, they trained other pilots to fly—and fight. They tested new and newly repaired aircraft to make sure they were safe enough for combat in the war zones. They flew thousands of warplanes across the country, transporting supplies and equipment. They even helped United States ground troops learn to fire at enemy planes in the air by towing targets for live gunnery practice. In all, they flew more than 60 million miles in 78 different types of military aircraft during the war. Thirty-eight of these pilots even lost their lives in the line of duty.

What was so unusual about these pilots?

They were women! And they made up the Women's Airforce Service Pilots—the WASPs. More than 1,000 of them trained at Avenger Field near Sweetwater, Texas, and they formed the first group of women pilots ever trained and deployed in a military effort.

Their experiences were unique. Their actions were brave and daring. They wanted to serve their country, and they served it well.

This is the story of the American WASPs.

The Flying WASPs of World War II
WOMEN'S AIRFORCE SERVICE PILOTS

(1942–1944)

It was 1944. The pilot at the controls of the World War II fighter plane was in trouble. Something was dangerously wrong.

Immediately after takeoff, the plane began pulling violently to the right. The pilot jammed down the left rudder pedal and threw the stick to the left, trying to bring the plane back to a level position. But the plane still felt as if it would cartwheel to the right—and crash. The plane's right wing had been damaged in combat earlier, but it had just been repaired. What could be wrong now?

"This could be it," the pilot whispered desperately, as the plane continued its rightward lurches. "If I don't think fast, it's all over."

One more chance, the pilot thought. "If I can push all my weight on the stick and force it left, I may make it."

The pilot heaved once again to the left. Then the plane began turning slowly, circling back to the landing field. It was still listing severely to the right, but it remained in the air. Perhaps there was hope after all.

When the plane was directly over the runway, the pilot cut off the power. The engine sputtered for a minute. Then there was silence. The pilot pushed the nose of the aircraft toward the ground, and the plane glided down and landed with a thud onto the concrete runway.

The pilot was shaken, but alive, and anxious to find out what had gone wrong.

The pilot hopped out of the plane to inspect its right side. What was the problem?

One look under the plane's right wing revealed the answer. A careless mechanic had hammered his tool box to the right wing! This mistake nearly took the pilot's life!

Although the pilot was used to danger, this was a close call. But the work had to be done. Each day pilots had to test as many as 10 newly repaired planes to make sure they were safe enough to go back into combat. And this pilot had volunteered to help—no matter what the risk.

This pilot's name was Gwen Clinksdale. She was a member of the Women's Airforce Service Pilots—the WASPs. And she was just doing her job.

THE FLYING WASPS

Gwen Clinksdale was one of the more than 25,000 American women who volunteered to join the WASPs.

Famed aviator and test pilot Jacqueline Cochran had persuaded the American military to set up a special corps of women pilots to assist the war effort. She reasoned that if women took over the essential domestic military flying jobs— like ferrying training planes from site to site and test-flying—more men could be free to fly in combat areas.

The United States Army Air Force agreed to the experiment and got Jacqueline Cochran to organize the effort in 1942. They established a training facility at Avenger Field near Sweetwater, Texas. Cochran issued a plea for volunteers from among the nation's already-licensed female pilots. And she was overwhelmed with the response.

Women were eager to assist the war effort, but there were few opportunities for them to do so. Thousands of women had taken jobs in arms production factories. Others had volunteered for duty with the Women's Army Corps (WACs) and the Women Accepted for Voluntary Emergency Services (WAVES). Still others had become Red Cross volunteers. But female pilots had no opportunity for service until Jacqueline Cochran organized the WASPs.

Cochran established rigid physical and mental entrance tests to insure that only the best pilots were accepted. She set up a six months training program, identical to what men received. Her standards were so high, and the training so difficult, that only 1,074 pilots completed the program.

Cochran wanted to make sure her young women pilots were not distracted, so she put the base "off limits" to all men, except for essential military personnel. Dating between the women pilots and the male instructors was forbidden. Soldiers joked that Avenger Field had become "Cochran's Convent." But the WASPs were no joke.

More than 1,000 women pilots trained at Avenger Field near Sweetwater, Texas, between 1942 and 1944.

WASP trainees spent part of the day in the classroom learning meteorology, electronics, aerodynamics, physics and navigation. Then they headed to the airfield for actual flight training.

BOOT CAMP

They were out of bed at 6:15 a.m.

They jumped into drab flight suits which had belonged to male pilots and were several sizes too big. They put bandanas on their heads. There was no time for makeup and hair-curlers.

At 7:30 sharp, half the group stood on the flight line waiting for flight instruction. The other half hit the books.

This was "boot camp," or the Army Air Force version of military training for the WASPs. It was just as rigorous as the training that male pilots faced.

Women who had studied art or fashion in school now learned physics, aerodynamics, electronics and instruments, engine operation and maintenance. They learned meteorology, navigation and military and civilian air regulations.

In the afternoon, the classroom students took their turns flying the training planes. At five in the afternoon, the groups came together for marching drills and calisthenics. For all this, they were paid $165 a month.

All the WASP trainees were pilots, but few had ever flown anything more powerful than a 60 horsepower aircraft. Now they had to learn to fly a 175 horsepower military training plane. It wasn't easy.

Even West Texas itself proved challenging to them.

The first thing the women did before each flight was to check their open cockpits for snakes!

The women had to learn to land in devilish crosswinds and to dodge the tiny dust cyclones that could tip a wing and cause a plane to crash. They learned to look out for tumbleweed that could become entangled in the landing gear or entwined in the propeller.

The WASP trainees received no special consideration because they were women. The flight instructors treated the women just like they treated the men—they yelled at them a lot!

Virginia Streeter, a 28-year-old nutritionist from New York, was determined to take it without complaining.

On her first flight, she put on her helmet and earphones and climbed into the front seat. Her instructor sat behind her in the open-cockpit plane. He shouted instructions through her earphones.

"Power-on stall. Power-off stall," he yelled.

Virginia complied. But every time she did what he told her, the instructor yelled out another order and criticized her violently.

"Pull the nose higher," he barked.

"Too much rudder."

"More rudder."

With every command or criticism, Virginia became more nervous. Finally her nervousness turned to anger.

When the instructor disliked one of her turns, he shouted out, "How can you be so dumb?"

That was too much for Virginia.

She was not dumb!

She tore off her helmet and earphones, throttled back to quiet the engine, and almost stood up in her seat as she leaned out of the cockpit to turn around to face the instructor.

"Stop being so smart," she shouted. "I'm doing the best I can."

The instructor looked dumbfounded. Then he grinned. He never yelled at her again.

Soon, the women were soloing in their small trainers.

The open-air cockpits offered a delightful break from the summer heat. But during the West Texas winters, the women were numb with cold. They had to wear fleece-lined jackets, gloves, goggles and helmets to keep warm. And these were always too big!

The WASPs were organized so quickly that no one really thought about uniforms for the women. They wore Army-issue men's flight suits and simply rolled up the pants legs or belted the suits tightly around their waists to make them fit. Even though their flying won raves, their appearance left much to be desired. Some military officers were so embarrassed when a group of army brass was coming to inspect the WASPs, that they sent the women into Sweetwater on a shopping spree to find "military-looking" clothing. The women came back with white blouses, khaki pants and turbans for their heads. These makeshift uniforms lasted until the army finally issued a special uniform for the WASPs in 1944.

GRADUATION

As soon as a WASP completed the difficult six-month training program, she was sent out to one of the many U.S. Army airfields across the country. Her assignment included whatever flying was required to help with the military operation.

Although the WASPs were technically civilians and not officially members of the U.S. Army Air Force, they were subject to military rules and regulations—as well as to the tough army discipline! The women were usually treated as officers, however, even though they had no official rank.

Many traditional military men thought these "girl pilots" were a novelty. They didn't really take them seriously. Other military officers acted downright hostile.

Target pilot Dolores Meurer found out first-hand about hostility in 1944. During her first week at a training base, she sat down for dinner at a table in the officers' mess. Several fighter pilots and the base commanding officer were already seated. Soon a waiter appeared behind her chair and told her the commanding officer requested she sit at another table. Delores was afraid she had violated some military custom by sitting at the table with the officers, and she got up to leave. Then she heard the commanding officer say, "I will not have a woman at my dinner table. It's unmilitary."

The only thing Dolores had violated was the prejudiced attitude of the commanding officer!

Some officers may have thought it was unmilitary for a female pilot to eat dinner with them. But few thought it was unmilitary when the women risked their lives training army troops to shoot moving targets.

WASPs established an outstanding safety record when they flew more than 60 million miles in 78 different types of aircraft for the World War II effort.

By 1944, most male pilots simply refused to pull target planes anymore. This was the process of having a pilot tow an aerial target behind the plane so that gunners on the ground could practice shooting at a moving target. It was the only way gunners could get the experience necessary to make them effective in combat situations. It was dangerous work. The inexperienced gunners often missed their target and hit the plane that towed it! Male pilots felt that if they were going to die, they wanted to do so in combat — and not by being shot at by their own men!

So for all practical purposes, this kind of target training stopped.

One day in 1944, the soldiers at Camp Irwin in California were ordered back into the training area. From the direction of the camp, a target airplane headed their way. The men began shooting enthusiastically.

After a while, the lieutenant in command heard his ground-to-air radio crackle. Then he heard a woman's voice: "Three holes in the tail, boys, that's a little close!" she said.

A woman was flying the target plane!

The WASPs made it possible for this kind of essential military training to continue.

They also transported planes, supplies and soldiers back and forth across the country. They tested airplanes to get them ready for combat duty. All in all they flew 78 different types of aircraft. They flew every kind of wartime mission that did not involve direct confrontation with enemy troops. They flew 60 million miles and established a lower accident rate than the male pilots who flew similar domestic missions. Nevertheless, 38 WASPs lost their lives in service flying.

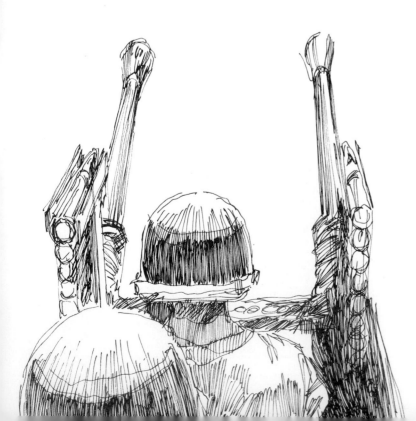

WHO JOINED THE WASPS?

Why would any young woman want to become a military pilot? Why would a young woman risk her life for her country when she could remain safely at home? Why would a woman choose danger and discomfort?

There were several reasons.

Patriotism. A sense of adventure. A desire to help. A need to use valuable skills and talents. These are qualities that some women, as well as some men, hold. Women who joined the WASPs had them all. They were patriotic, adventurous, skilled and eager to help. And more.

"I just wanted to fly," said one WASP B-17 pilot.

These women had been trained to fly, yet many of them felt that their skills and talents were wasted—unless they could contribute to the effort to win the war by flying!

Who were these women?

Most were young and well-educated. Some were debutantes and actresses. Others were students, secretaries and scientists. They included:

- Jacqueline Cochran, the director of the WASPs, was one of the most accomplished pilots in aviation history. It was she who persuaded the Commanding General of the Army Air Force, "Hap" Arnold, to establish the WASP program. General Arnold named her director of all women pilots in the Army Air Force in 1943. Jacqueline later flew military jets and participated in the planning of the U.S. space program. In 1953, Jacqueline Cochran became the first woman to break the sound barrier, at a speed of 652.337 miles per hour. Eleven years later, she doubled that speed at a record-shattering 1,429.2 miles per hour! She competed in air races and was the first woman to win the prestigious Bendix International Race. Cochran also holds the distinction of having set more aviation records than any other pilot, male or female.
- Gwen Clinksdale, the test pilot, was a biologist from North Carolina.
- Helen Dettweiler was a professional golfer.

- Helen Richey was the first woman commercial airline pilot.
- Margaret Kerr was a member of the oil-rich Kerr family from Oklahoma.
- Marion Florsheim was heiress to a shoe business fortune.
- Mildred Davidson was a secretary from Austin, Texas, who enlisted in the WASPs after she found out that her military husband was missing-in-action.
- Dr. Dora Strother was a pilot who later set world records as a helicopter pilot and won awards as an aviation psychologist.

And there were many, many more outstanding young women who became a part of the historic WASP effort.

There was something special about all of them.

"They were leaders," one veteran said. "They were willing to push themselves forward when it would have been a lot easier to sit around and do nothing."

The women who joined the WASPs were young, well educated and eager to help their country.

THE WASPS ARE GROUNDED

All through the war, the WASPs looked forward to the day when they would become official members of the U.S. Army Air Force and receive full military rank and benefits.

They proved that they could do a "man's job"—and in some cases do it even better than the men.

"It is on the record that women fly as well as men," said General "Hap" Arnold.

Instead of the reward of military rank, however, members of the WASPs received a stunning blow. Without warning, the entire program was closed down in December 1944!

The war effort was coming to a close. The United States and its allies were close to victory.

The spectacular air battles in Europe were ending. Fewer and fewer male pilots were needed for combat operations. Many pilots had been assigned to ground units, and they were keenly disappointed that they could no longer fly. Pressure mounted on military officials to allow some of these men to take over the domestic flying duties performed so admirably by the WASPs.

"Let the men come home and do the jobs the women have done," they urged.

And that is what happened. The Army Air Force disbanded the WASPs. Their training, testing and ferrying missions were taken over by the male pilots. The WASPs were told to go home.

And no one gave them much of an official "thank you," either. Other veterans of World War II service, including men who had never seen combat, received tremendous benefits for their service—financial aid for education, housing and health care. The United States Army did not even pay tribute to the WASPs who were killed in action. The parents of these women had to pay to bring their daughters' bodies home.

Memories of their brief and glorious service were all that remained for more than 1,000 women who served their country bravely during World War II. Memories—and pride!

The WASPs were so proud of their service record that they decided to band together after the war to see if they could get some official recognition from the United States Congress. They wrote letters to members of Congress. They made trips to Washington. They issued press releases and appeared on television talk shows. They did everything possible to draw public attention to the valuable services they provided to the nation during World War II. Finally, they succeeded. On May 8, 1979, the United States Secretary of Defense announced that the wartime service of the WASPs would be considered "active military duty."

The WASPs were at last considered military veterans, with all rights and benefits.

The United States Air Force issued the first honorable discharge to a WASP—35 years after the war.

The WASPs still have an active organization, and its members work as airline officials, nurses, judges, housewives, business executives and more.

They are still very special people.

Bell Helicopter Textron, Ft. Worth

WASPS' SONG

We are Yankee Doodle Pilots
Yankee Doodle do or die
Real live nieces of our Uncle Sam
Born with a yearning to fly
Keep in step to all our classes
March to flight line with our pals
Yankee Doodle came to Texas
Just to fly the "PTs"
We are those Yankee Doodle Gals!

Former WASP Dr. Dora Strother set the world helicopter altitude record for female pilots in 1961. Like Dr. Strother, many WASP veterans continued aviation careers. Others became lawyers, teachers, businesswomen, housewives and nurses.

America's First Female Astronauts
SPACE WOMEN

NASA

Right. America's first eight women astronauts, from top left, clockwise: Mary Cleave, Bonnie Dunbar, Judith Resnik, Anna Fisher, Kathryn Sullivan, Rhea Seddon, Sally Ride and Shannon Lucid.
Far right. All astronauts—men and women—had to complete one year of rigorous training to become eligible for space flight.

America entered the space age in 1961 when the Redstone rocket hurled the tiny Mercury capsule and its passenger, Alan Shepard, into space for a brief 15 minutes. It took only eight more years for America to put a man on the moon and enter a whole new era of sophisticated space exploration.

America's first astronauts — our first travelers and workers in space — were all men. The first group of astronauts — John Glenn, Wally Schirra, Gordon Cooper, Scott Carpenter, Gus Grissom, Alan Shepard and Deke Slayton — became national heroes. Americans stayed tuned to their television sets to watch the astronauts' dramatic space launches and perilous returns to Earth. Former test pilots or military officers, these first astronauts were considered among the bravest and most daring of America's long list of heroes. Later, moon-walkers Neil Armstrong, Alan Bean and others added to the image of astronauts as tough, smart and brave men. And they were. They carried out dangerous work and new ventures into unknown worlds.

These early space explorers also performed hundreds of scientific, technical and physical experiments in space. They determined the limits of their own endurance, as well as the safety and uses of their space equipment.

In addition to exciting discoveries, their experiments led them to a simple conclusion: you don't have to be a man to be an astronaut.

In the weightless, or zero-gravity, conditions of space, strength and size made very little difference. In fact, smaller individuals had more room to maneuver in the sometimes-cramped space cabin environment.

The astronauts and other officials with the National Aeronautics and Space Administration (NASA) discovered exactly what would be required for space travel in the late 20th and early 21st centuries. Astronauts would have to be intelligent, flexible, resourceful, healthy and able to cope with stressful situations — including the possibility of death. Men did not have a monopoly on those traits!

When NASA began recruiting astronauts in 1977, the first time since Neil Armstrong walked on the moon in 1969, officials for the first time encouraged women to apply. And they did. More than 1,000 of the 8,000 applicants were women. And of the 35 new astronauts selected for training in 1978, six were women. In 1980, two more women were added to the program.

Women's entry into the space program paralleled their entry into all kinds of non-traditional jobs, a result of efforts to secure full legal and economic opportunities for women. The age of new opportunities for women coincided with the age of new opportunities for space travel.

Our imagination allows us to visualize space colonies where people live and work, and commute to Earth on regular shuttle flights. It may take many years to make this possible. But the work is started. And we already know that if there are to be settlements in space, they will include women as well as men.

Women have already begun to participate in this glorious adventure. This is the story of the first eight women to enter America's space program. They will not be the last.

They were pretty enough to win beauty contests.

They were smart enough to have the best jobs in their professions.

They were determined enough to become successful at anything they wanted to do.

And what *did* they want to do?

They wanted to fly — in space!

The first eight women astronauts might have dreamed about soaring among the stars. They might have wanted to feel that powerful surge of energy as huge booster rockets lifted their spacecraft into orbit. Perhaps they wanted to wear those life-supporting spacesuits, with the American flag stitched on their sleeves. Or perhaps they wanted to see their home — the "wondrous" planet Earth — from out in space, as only a few humans had been able to do.

For various reasons they wanted to join in the grand adventure of space exploration and discovery. They wanted to be part of the future!

Even though these first space women nurtured their dreams over the years, they had little hope of becoming astronauts. After all, the American astronauts had always been men! Yet, without fully abandoning their dreams, each began to develop skills which might allow her to participate in the new kinds of space travel America would almost certainly undertake.

Mary Cleave, Bonnie Dunbar, Anna Fisher, Shannon Lucid, Judith Resnik, Sally Ride, Rhea Seddon and Kathryn Sullivan began to prepare for the future. Some of these women became pilots. All eight became scientists, physicians or engineers. They were ready.

But they had to wait. It was not until the development of the space shuttle program in the 1970s that they had the opportunity to fulfill their dreams.

The National Aeronautics and Space Administration (NASA) had developed a shuttle spacecraft that could carry heavy loads into space. It could also return to Earth to be used again and again.

This meant that valuable scientific experiments could be conducted in space and returned to Earth for analysis.

It meant that satellites could be repaired in space or returned to Earth in the shuttle spacecraft.

It even meant that products could be manufactured in space. The shuttle could transport raw materials and finished goods.

And it also meant that large solar power stations and self-sustaining space colonies could be built by spacesuited construction crews. The shuttle could make scheduled trips into space, just like airplanes, trains and trucks do on Earth. The new vehicle was remarkable.

"It takes off like a rocket, maneuvers in Earth orbit like a spacecraft and lands like an airplane," NASA said of the shuttle, which could swing around the Earth in orbits from 100 to 300 miles above the surface.

NASA officials were excited. They called the space shuttle a true aerospace vehicle. And the pioneer shuttle, *Columbia*, thrilled Americans — and the world — with its first flight in 1981.

NASA had to recruit a new kind of astronaut for the shuttle program. And for the first time, NASA encouraged women as well as men to apply. The new shuttle astronauts would have to be more than test pilots. They would have to have a broad range of scientific and practical knowledge. And because it cost NASA between $8 million and $10 million to train and keep an astronaut in the program over a 10 or 15 year period, NASA had to be certain that the people it selected could handle a wide variety of jobs.

NASA began looking for people with solid technical backgrounds in science, engineering or medicine. It wanted people who had the discipline to work on a number of different projects in space. And it wanted people who could tolerate extremely stressful and difficult situations — including the possibility of serious injury or even death.

NASA found the people it was looking for. People like Mary, Bonnie, Kathy, Anna, Shannon, Sally, Rhea and Judy. These women, and others, finally had the opportunity to join America's space program. And space program officials were delighted with the new women and men who formed the 78-member astronaut corps for the 1980s.

"They represented the cream of the crop of human beings," according to Christopher Kraft,

Jr., director of the Lyndon B. Johnson Space Center in Houston.

The work of these celebrated astronauts included conducting scientific experiments and co-ordinating a whole range of activities that would take place in the space shuttle's cargo bay — the 60-foot-long storage area large enough to carry a school bus. It was here that massive doors, which covered the entire length of the cargo bay, could be opened to space so that a satellite might be launched or repaired. It was here also that experiments could be conducted. And it was here that the shuttle's gigantic mechanical arm might pick up a large item and send it overboard.

The astronauts who coordinated those activities were called "mission specialists." And they had work to do, even when they weren't scheduled for a trip into space. Mission specialists had helped on all of the shuttle launches at Cape Canaveral. They had flown simulated ascents and descents in the shuttle lab to work out any kinks in the shuttle's computer system. They had learned to do just about everything that anyone could do in space.

Some called the mission specialists "space age repairmen." But some of America's space repair-*men* were women!

What was so special about America's space women — the first females to come to the Lyndon B. Johnson Space Center in Houston, Texas, to train as astronauts? Who were they?

> *Many people around here (NASA) had in their minds that these would be women doing men's jobs. I know I thought that. Astronauts, to me, were men; they had to think about computers and spaceship flying — male things. But I've changed that opinion. The job of astronaut is just as female as it is male. Females intuitively understand astronaut skills. They perform the mental and physical tasks as well as males do.*
>
> —Alan Bean, astronaut veteran of 1,671 hours in space and lunar module pilot of Apollo 12, quoted in *Texas Monthly*

Astronaut exercises ranged from maneuvering in the space-like weightless conditions of a water tank to concentrating on space flights at Mission Control.

NASA

NASA

MARY CLEAVE, PhD (b. 1947)

NASA

Mary had wanted to fly ever since her parents took her to an Air Force base on Armed Forces Day when she was a little girl.

"Boy, I'd like to fly one of these babies," she said when she examined a sleek Air Force jet.

"You'll never fly one of these, young lady," said an airman standing nearby.

But that airman didn't know Mary Cleave. She learned to fly an airplane before she learned to drive a car. Mary's mother would drive her to flying lessons; then Mary would take her mother up in the airplane for a little spin.

Mary loved flying so much that she wanted to make a career of it. But few commercial flying jobs existed for women, so Mary decided she'd become an airline stewardess. At barely five feet, two inches tall, Mary was too short to do even that. So she studied biology in college to become a teacher, like her mother.

Mary also began to develop a growing concern about the pollution of our nation's rivers and lakes, and she decided to do something about it. She became one of the first women at Utah State University to earn a Ph.D. degree in engineering, and then she worked to solve waste disposal problems.

But Mary had not forgotten about flying. Mary had been only 16 years old when the Russians had sent the first woman into space in 1963. Like many girls, she probably wondered, "why not me?" And she held onto her dream to fly. When NASA began recruiting new astronauts for the space program in 1977, Mary applied.

"Mary knew that her chances of being selected by NASA were slim . . . but the more she learned about the space shuttle program the more she wanted to be a part of it," wrote Lawrence Wright in *Texas Monthly* magazine.

Her chances were indeed slim at that time. Mary was among the almost 8,000 applicants who NASA turned down. But she didn't give up. Because NASA had already selected six women for the program, Mary still hoped that someday she might be chosen. After all, the space program was going to need technical specialists, like herself, and so Mary worked to sharpen her professional skills. Mary applied to NASA again in 1980, and this time she was one of two additional women accepted into the nation's elite corps of astronauts.

Survival courses prepared astronaut candidates for emergencies during their jet training flights. Mary Cleave mastered simulated—and real—parachute jumps.

BONNIE J. DUNBAR (b. 1949)

Bonnie Dunbar worked on the space shuttle long before she became an astronaut. As a senior engineer with a private aerospace firm in California, Bonnie helped develop equipment and processes for manufacturing the space shuttle's thermal protection system. This system included the tiles on the shuttle's surface which protected it from the extreme heat generated when the craft hurtled through the atmosphere on its way back to Earth.

Bonnie liked what she saw of the shuttle and decided she wanted to be involved in its grand space adventure. So she went to work for NASA in 1978 as a guidance and navigation officer. And she got even more deeply involved in the space program when she served as a flight controller for the Skylab re-entry mission in 1979. Later, she coordinated several space shuttle payload operations.

After all of this, it seemed only natural for Bonnie to become one of the two woman added to the astronaut corps in 1980. She was more than ready for the challenge.

Bonnie had always thrived on challenges. She grew up on a farm in Washington State and was driving a tractor by the time she was nine years old. She learned to handle her share of the family farm responsibilities and developed a strong sense of self-confidence in the process.

Bonnie continued to find challenges — and then to meet them. She learned to fly airplanes. In college, she entered the difficult field of ceramic engineering. She graduated with honors from the Uni-

NASA

versity of Washington and received a NASA graduate research grant in 1973 and 1974.

Bonnie credited her parents with helping her make her way into the space program. They taught her that she could do anything that she wanted. It didn't make any difference whether she was a girl or a boy. The world was hers to conquer — as long as she had the determination.

The first women astronauts attracted widespread media publicity. Camera crews closely followed Bonnie Dunbar as she completed her water survival training course.

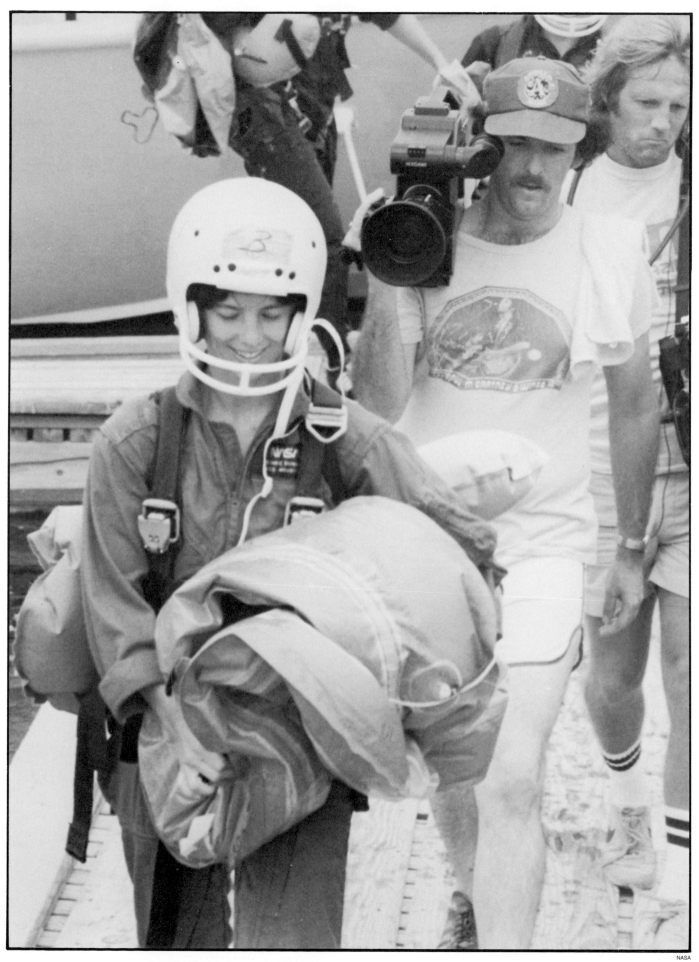

ANNA FISHER, MD (b. 1949)

NASA

Anna Fisher and her husband Bill applied together to the NASA astronaut program in 1977. They were both physicians who specialized in emergency medicine.

Bill had entered the field in order to prepare himself to become an astronaut — a dream of his since he was 12 years old. It was a dream that Anna had for herself, too. But she had very little hope that she would be selected, and Bill had to persuade her to apply. As it turned out, NASA selected Anna to become an astronaut — not Bill!

Anna worried as much about her husband's rejection as she rejoiced about her own selection.

"I wanted to retain my enthusiasm, but I didn't want to see Bill hurt," she said.

But Bill was proud of Anna. "Heck, to have one astronaut in the family — you can't complain about that," he said. Bill applied to the program again in 1980, and this time he was accepted. He and Anna became NASA's first husband and wife astronaut team.

Anna's background in chemistry and her specialty in the field of emergency medicine made her a choice pick for the astronaut program. If there was one place where serious medical emergencies could arise, it was certainly in space.

But even more critical to Anna was the opportunity to conduct medical research experiments in the space shuttle's payload area, which could be outfitted as a fully equipped scientific laboratory. Research in the sterile and weightless conditions of space could prove extremely important to advance the knowledge and techniques of emergency medicine on Earth. As a mission specialist, Dr. Anna Fisher would be conducting some of those experiments.

Anna Fisher, shown here enjoying a moment of weightlessness in an Air Force cargo plane, was one of the first physicians selected as a mission specialist for the space shuttle program.

NASA

SHANNON LUCID, PhD (b. 1943)

Shannon Lucid was born in China where her parents were missionaries. And it was the experience of flying high over the mountains of China when she was only five years old that prompted Shannon's passionate love of flying.

Many years later, after Shannon had returned to the United States and learned to fly, she tried her best to become a commercial airline pilot. She submitted her application to nearly every airline in the United States in the 1960s, and was turned down by every one of them. Women simply could not get top-paying jobs flying airplanes. Nevertheless, she managed to log more than 1,700 hours of instrument, commercial and multi-engine flying time.

Shannon also had other skills. And she decided to make good use of them. She studied biochemistry in college and received her Ph.D. from the University of Oklahoma. While Shannon was earning her professional credentials in college, she was also busy being a wife and mother. Shannon and her husband Michael had three children.

After college, Shannon worked as a chemist for an oil company and conducted research with the Oklahoma Medical Research Foundation. When she decided to apply for the space program, her husband supported her decision and offered to give up his job to move to Texas with her.

The Lucid family was enthusiastic about the move once Shannon became an astronaut candidate in 1978. In fact, Shannon's children thought

NASA

they'd get to go along with her when she traveled in space. After all, their family always did *everything* together!

But Shannon, the first American mother accepted into the space program, was looking to an even more distant future.

In an interview in *Newsweek*, she said, "Wouldn't it be great when I'm old and gray to be able to lean back in my rocking chair and remember when I was out taking a stroll among the stars?"

Flying wasn't new to Astronaut Shannon Lucid. She was an experienced pilot, and biochemist, before she entered the space program.

JUDITH RESNIK, PhD

(b. 1949)

Judith Resnik was the kind of calm, matter-of-fact young professional NASA was looking for in the space shuttle program.

George Abbey, director of flight operations at the Johnson Space Center, wanted astronauts who could be focused, patient and flexible.

That was Judith. Trained as an electrical engineer, with a Ph.D. from the University of Maryland, Judith worked for a while as a design engineer at RCA. There, she helped develop custom integrated circuitry for radar control systems. It was complicated, tedious work.

Later, Judith shifted her area of interest to medical research. She served as a biomedical engineer and worked on biological research experiments at the National Institute of Health in Maryland. Again, it was difficult work.

Judith took it all in stride. And it was that kind of detailed, methodical work that prepared her for the space program. After all, being an astronaut would not be all glamour and space-walks. There would be many small, routine jobs that had to be carefully completed each day. There would be complications, details, long hours and repetitious testing—just like any job.

Judith had a sense of adventure. But she was also extremely serious about her work. She specialized in work on the shuttle's mechanical arm, the remote control system that could pluck a satellite from orbit or put building materials into space.

"Progress in science is as exciting to me as sitting in a rocket is to some people," she said.

Judith Resnik, like many astronauts of the 1980s, was drawn to the space program as much by the possibility of scientific discovery as by the lure of pure adventure.

SALLY RIDE, PhD (b. 1951)

"It's your basic once-in-a-lifetime opportunity," astrophysicist Sally Ride said about becoming an astronaut.

"Thirty years from now when they're selling round-trip tickets to Mars, this might not be glamorous," she said. But for the 1980s, Sally was awfully glad to be part of the space shuttle program.

Sally was born and raised in Encino, California where her father taught psychology and her mother taught college English. When she was a teenager, Sally was a nationally-ranked junior tennis player. She continued her interest in sports by jogging and playing rugby, volleyball and softball.

Sally's athletic ability and her special skills as a laser-physicist made her uniquely qualified to be an astronaut. There was only one time when she had a doubt.

During the ocean survival exercises in the first stages of astronaut training, Sally—and all the astronaut candidates—were tested to the limit. After being hooked up to a rope pulled by a motorboat, Sally was dragged through the water. Then she was dropped 400 feet down into a swamp. Next, she had to slide down a 45-foot tower into mosquito-infested water. And that wasn't all. She had to await ocean rescue while drifting alone in a tiny raft in choppy seas.

"What am I doing here? I'm supposed to be a smart person," Sally thought.

Well, Sally was smart. And she got through the tough physical training well enough to qualify as an astronaut mission specialist.

Many television viewers got used to seeing—and hearing—Sally when she served as an on-orbit capsule communicator for some of the early space shuttle missions.

Fellow astronaut, Lieutenant Colonel John M. Fabian, commented in a *GEO* magazine interview: "Sally is driven by a desire to do what's right and to learn what's necessary"

Sally Ride's athletic ability and specialty as a laser-physicist made her uniquely qualified to be a space shuttle astronaut.

U.S. AIR FORCE T-38A
A.F. SERIAL NO. (59)

RHEA SEDDON, MD (b. 1947)

Rhea Seddon always liked to be first. She wanted to be in on the beginnings of things. If she hadn't become one of America's first women astronauts, she probably would have been one of the first physicians to enter the new medical field of intravenous nutrition.

In July 1982, Rhea achieved another "first" when she became the first astronaut to give birth to a baby. She and her astronaut husband, Robert L. Gibson, became the proud parents of Paul Seddon Gibson.

Rhea continued working in the space program right up until the birth of her son. And she went back to work after the baby was born.

Rhea always wanted to be an astronaut. But she didn't know if that were possible.

"I didn't know if the space program would ever be open to women," Rhea said. "So I decided to become a doctor so that even if I never did get a chance, I would be able to lead a meaningful life."

Rhea completed her general surgery residency in Memphis and developed a consuming interest in surgical nutrition. Later, she conducted research into the effects of radiation therapy on nutrition in cancer patients.

Rhea's interest in nutrition and the effect of special diets on human health coincided with NASA's interest. Many of the space program's early experiments with food technology and packaging techniques have been used outside the space program to help provide balanced meals to people who are ill, or to the elderly who live alone.

As a mission specialist, Rhea would get the opportunity to continue some of her nutrition research.

NASA

Like many of the astronauts, Rhea acknowledged her parents for helping her make it into the program.

"Mother gave me a love of books and the quiet inward things, and Dad always encouraged me to try new activities," Rhea said.

Perhaps the most important thing Rhea's dad told her was that she could "go anywhere in the world . . . if she really wanted to."

Rhea has proved him correct.

Rhea Seddon brought unique self confidence to her combined careers as an astronaut and a mother. She and her husband, Astronaut Robert Gibson, became the first "astronaut parents" when their baby, Paul Seddon Gibson, was born in 1982.

KATHRYN D. SULLIVAN, PhD

(b.1951)

NASA

Kathryn Sullivan once set an unofficial altitude record for women by flying at 63,300 feet.

But Kathy was just as comfortable on the water as she was in the air. As a marine geophysicist, she spent many hours as a seagoing scientist, conducting research in oceans all over the world. In fact, she found many similarities between her ocean voyages and space travel.

"Being 500 miles at sea is very similar to a space mission," she said.

Kathy probably thought loading up a shuttle orbiter with instruments and flying into space would be a whole lot like loading a ship with marine research tools and setting out to sea.

But Kathy found one major difference in the space program. In a space vehicle, everything had to be planned, down to the last tiny detail. And although this required tremendous discipline, Kathy loved the challenge.

Once she joined the space program, Kathy specialized in spaceborn remote sensing, which would allow spacecraft to identify and locate other objects in outer space. Her research led her to work on several remote sensing projects in Alaska.

Kathy also qualified as a systems engineer operator in one of NASA's special high-altitude research aircraft.

Kathy's love of the ocean and her yearning for space flying were balanced equally with her love of the Earth itself. An ardent environmentalist, she worried about pollution of the Earth's resources.

"I don't want to be an astronaut just because we mucked up down here and need to run away from the mess," Kathy said. "Space exploration works as long as it's not a substitute for taking care of the Earth."

If Kathy has her way, we'll have the best of *all* worlds.

Kathryn Sullivan set an unofficial sustained altitude record for women when she flew at 63,300 feet in 1979 aboard this high-altitude jet.

"My mother never warned me not to do this or that for fear of being hurt. Of course I got hurt, but I was never afraid."

—Katherine Stinson

Notes on Sources and Additional Facts

We Can Fly — Katherine Stinson

The main source for direct quotations appearing in the story was an article that Katherine Stinson wrote, "Why I am Not Afraid to Fly," published in *The American Magazine* in 1917. Sources for facts about her flying feats included *The Stinsons*, by John Underwood (Glendale, Calif.: Heritage Press, 1969), and *Heroines of the Sky*, by Jean Adams and Margaret Kimball (Garden City, NY: Doubleday, 1942). Other sources consulted were "Katherine Stinson, 'The Flying Schoolgirl,'" *FAA Aviation News*, November 1971; Lester Zaiontz, "Stinson Field," *San Antonio Reporter*, 6 May 1976; and "Sky-Sign Made by Girl Flyer," *Los Angeles Times*, 18 December 1915.

Marjorie Stinson sidebar

The information about Marjorie Stinson was found primarily in newspaper articles. These articles included: "Marjorie Stinson, 79, Dies: Pioneer Air Mail Pilot," *Washington Star*, 18 April 1975; Lester Zaiontz, "Stinson Field," *San Antonio Reporter*, 13 May 1976; "Air Unit Honors Stinsons," *San Antonio Express-News*, 7 Nov. 1964; obituary, *San Antonio News*, 4 June 1975. Other sources included "Youngest Flyer in America: a San Antonio Girl," *Aerial Age Weekly*, 17 April 1916; "Wings for War Birds," *Liberty*, 28 Dec. 1929; and "Stinson Municipal Airport, 1916–1980" (San Antonio: Stinson Field, 1980).

Texas Heroine: Katherine Stinson
Born: Fort Payne, Alabama, 1891
Died: Santa Fe, New Mexico, 1977
Most Notable Accomplishments: Fourth licensed woman pilot in U.S., 1912
First woman authorized to fly the mail, 1913
First woman pilot to loop-the-loop, 1915
First woman pilot to skywrite at night, 1915
Holder of speed and distance records
First woman pilot to perform in the Orient, 1916
Family Status: Married Miguel A. Otero, Jr., attorney and judge, in 1928
No children
Personal Characteristics: Spunky, energetic, known as "Flying School-girl" for her youthful appearance

Texas Heroine: Marjorie Stinson
Born: Fort Payne, Alabama, 1896
Died: Washington, D.C., 1975
Most Notable Accomplishments: Ninth and youngest woman pilot licensed in U.S., 1914
First woman flight instructor, 1915
First pilot to fly air mail in Texas, 1915
First woman to serve in the U.S. Aviation Reserve Corps, 1915
Family Status: Never married; no children
Personal Characteristics: Small, plucky, quiet

W.D. Smithers Collection, Humanities Research Center, The University of Texas at Austin

Katherine Stinson liked driving fast cars as well as performing flying stunts.

The World's Greatest Athlete— Babe Didrikson Zaharias

A major source for this chapter was Babe Didrikson Zaharias's autobiography *This Life I've Led* (New York: A.S. Barnes & Co., 1955); Another important source was *'Whatta-Gal': The Babe Didrikson Story* by William Oscar Johnson and Nancy P. Williamson (Boston and Toronto: Little, Brown and Co., 1975). Additional sources included: Mary Kay Kneif, "The Babe" in Francis Edward Abernethy, ed., *Legendary Ladies of Texas* (Dallas: E-Heart Press, 1981); Frank Litsky, *Superstars* (Secaucus, N.J.; Derbibooks, Inc., 1975); and "Babe Didrikson Zaharias 1912–1956," *Official Motion Pictures Guinness Book of World Records* (New York: Big Fights, Inc., 1976).

Daring Doctor of Brazoria— Sofie Herzog

The most imporant sources for facts about Dr. Herzog's life were a series of articles by Marie Beth Jones in the Brazosport, Texas newspaper *Brazosport Facts*. They included: "Dr. Sofie Followed Daughter to Texas," 18 Jan. 1961; "Bullet Necklace a 'Lucky Piece'," 25 Jan. 1961; "Dr. Sofie Was Railroad Doctor," 1 Feb. 1961; "Office Exhibit A Bit Startling," 8 Feb. 1961; "Dr. Sofie Builds a Church," 16 Feb. 1961; "Sofie Combined Career, Family," 22 Feb. 1961. Other sources included a book by Mrs. George Plunkett Red, *Medicine Man in Texas* (Houston: Standard Printing, 1930) and an unpublished article by Adele Perry Caldwell, "Character Sketch of Dr. Sofie Herzog, Brazoria, Texas," in the Brazoria County Library, Angleton.

Reagan Bradshaw, Austin

The City of Chicago presented Babe Didrikson this trophy naming her "the world's greatest athlete—man or woman."

Texas Heroine: Babe Didrikson Zaharias
Born: Port Arthur, Texas, 1912
Died: Galveston, Texas, 1956
Most Notable Accomplishments: Greatest athlete of the first half of the 20th century
　　　Winner of more titles and records in more sports than any other athlete
　　　Winner of three individual Olympic medals, two gold and one silver, 1932
　　　Winner of every major women's golf championship, 1940–1950
Family Status: Married George Zaharias, wrestler and sports promoter, in 1938
　　　No children
Personal Characteristics: Humorous, brash, personable, competitive

---

Texas Heroine: Dr. Sophie Herzog
Born: Austria, 1848
Died: Brazoria, Texas, 1925
Most Notable Accomplishments: One of the first women to practice medicine in Texas, c. 1893
　　　First woman to serve as chief surgeon of a railroad in Texas, 1907
　　　Expert at removing bullets from gunshot victims
Family Status: Married Dr. Herzog, physician and surgeon, in 1862; widowed in 1888
　　　Married Marian Huntington, plantation owner, in 1913; widowed in 1924
　　　Mother of fourteen children
Personal Characteristics: Attractive, lively, determined.

The Director — Margo Jones

The primary source for this story was a book by Margo Jones, *Theatre-in-the-Round* (New York: Rinehart Publishing Co., 1951). Other sources included: Lyn Sher, *The American Women's Gazeteer* (New York: Bantam Books, 1976); Ronald L. Davis, "Jones, Margaret Virginia (Margo)," in E. S. Branda, ed., *The Handbook of Texas: A Supplement,* vol. 3 (Austin: Texas State Historical Association, 1976); a newspaper article by Wanda McDaniel, "Past Comes Full Circle," *Dallas Times Herald,* 14 Jan. 1975; and one by Don Safran, "Impact of a 25th Margo Jones Birthday," *Dallas Times Herald,* 18 June 1972; a "Theatre '47" program (Gulf Oil Theatre, 1947) in Margo Jones Collection, Dallas Public Library; a "Margo Jones Theater Festival" program (Texas Women's University, April 1982) in Texas Foundation for Women's Resources files, Austin; Jane Sumner, Ruthe Winegarten and Joyce Schiff, "Margo Jones" in Sketching Texas Women radio script, KERA-Dallas, 1975.

Savior of the Alamo — Clara Driscoll

A major source for this chapter was Martha Anne Turner's biography *Clara Driscoll: An American Tradition* (Austin: Madrona Press, 1979). Other sources included: a journal article by L. Robert Ables, "The Second Battle for the Alamo," *Southwest Historical Quarterly* vol. 70, no. 3 (1967); a pamphlet by Jack C. Butterfield, "Clara Driscoll Rescued the Alamo: A Brief Biography" (Daughters of the Republic of Texas, 1961); a letter from David Orr, Director of Development, Driscoll Foundation Children's Hospital, 18 Aug. 1980, to Sherry Smith, in Texas Foundation for Women's Resources files, Austin.

Driscoll Foundation, Corpus Christi

Clara Driscoll, circa 1910

Before she formed *La Cruz Blanca*, Leonor Magnon taught these kindergarten students in her Laredo home.

Texas Heroine: Jovita Idar
Born: Laredo, Texas, 1885
Died: San Antonio, Texas, 1946
Most Notable Accomplishments: Political activist and journalist
  who acted as advocate for Mexican-Americans in South Texas,
  1910s
  Founder of Mexican-American feminist organization, La Liga
  Femenil Mexicanista, 1911
Family Status: Married Bartolo Juarez, 1917
  No children
Personal Characteristics: Tall, dedicated, avid reader, intense

Texas Heroine: Leonor Villegas de Magnon
Born: Mexico, 1876
Died: Mexico City, Mexico, 1955
Most Notable Accomplishments: Founder of medical relief organiza-
  tion during Mexican Revolution, *La Cruz Blanca*, 1913
Family Status: Married Adolpho Magnon in 1901
  Mother of three children
Personal Characteristics: Small, spirited, persistent, fearless, known as
  La Rebelde (The Rebel)

Women of a Revolution — Jovita Idar and Leonor Villegas de Magnon

An important source on Jovita Idar was an unpublished paper by Jovita Lopez, Jovita Idar's niece, in the Texas Foundation for Women's Resources files, Austin. Another source in the Foundation's files is a letter from Jovita Lopez, 29 September 1981, to Janelle Scott. Janelle Scott also interviewed Jovita Lopez by telephone on 15 Sept. 1981. Other sources included: Anita Brenner, *The Wind That Swept Mexico* (Austin and London: University of Texas Press, 1971) and Martha Cotera, *Diosa y Hembra: The History and Heritage of Chicanas in the U.S.* (Austin: Information Systems Development, 1976); a magazine article by Jose E. Linom, "El Primer Congreso Mexicanista de 1911: A Precursor to Contemporary Chicanismo," *Aztlan*, Spring and Fall 1974; newspaper articles "A La Mujer Mexican de Ambos Laredos," *La Cronica*, 14 Sept. 1911, and "Battle in Nuevo Laredo," *Laredo Times*, March 1961.

Sources for facts about Leonor Villegas de Magnon included: a book by J. B. Wilkinson, *Laredo and the Rio Grande Frontier* (Austin: Jenkins Publishing Co., 1975); newspaper articles "Evolucion Mexicana," *La Cronica*, 7 Sept. 1911, "Rebel Forces Still Threatening Nuevo Laredo and Retain Ground," *Laredo Times*, 2 Jan. 1914, "Battle in Nuevo Laredo," *Laredo Times*, March 1961; a letter from Leonor Magnon Grubbs, the daughter of Leonor Villegas de Magnon, to Janelle Scott, 5 Jan. 1982, in Texas Foundation for Women's Resources files, Austin; a telephone interview with Leonor Magnon Grubbs by Sherry Smith, 22 April 1982.

Millionaire Inventor — Bette Graham

The main source for facts about Bette Graham's founding and developing the Liquid Paper Corporation was the Corporation publication *Letter Perfect*. Articles from *Letter Perfect* included "A History of the Liquid Paper Corporation," April 1980, and "Bette Graham Explains Her Philosophy," May 1980. The Liquid Paper Corporation files in Dallas provided the following sources: Bette Graham speech to New Enterprise Club, Harvard Business School, Harvard University, 9 March 1977; Bette Graham's "Founder's Report" to annual employee's meeting of the Liquid Paper Corporation, 24 May 1974; letter to Mistake Out Company from Leonore Hubbard Owens-Illinois, 17 Feb. 1959. Other sources included: a magazine article by Nancy Goebel, "The Unlimited Potential of Bette Graham," *Texas Woman*, July 1979; and a newspaper article "Bette Clair Graham, Inventor of Liquid Paper, Dies at 56," *Dallas Times Herald*, 14 May 1980.

Texas Heroine: Bette Graham
Born: San Antonio, Texas, 1924
Died: Dallas, Texas, 1980
Most Notable Accomplishments: Invented Liquid Paper correction fluid, 1951
　　Developed multimillion dollar Liquid Paper Corporation, 1960s and 1970s
　　Established two philanthropic foundations to assist women in business and the arts, Bette Clair McMurray Foundation in 1976 and Gihon Foundation in 1978
Family Status: Married Bob Graham, who joined her in the development of Liquid Paper Corp., in 1962; divorced in 1975
　　One son, Michael Nesmith, from prior marriage
Personal Characteristics: Tall, stately, quiet, artistic, devoted to Christian Science

---

Successful Suffragist — Jane Y. McCallum

The Jane Y. McCallum Papers in the Austin-Travis County Collection, Austin Public Library, were a valuable source for this story. Material used from the McCallum Papers included: Jane Y. McCallum's personal diary; an unpublished paper by Jane Y. McCallum, "An Old Timer Returns"; and a Texas Equal Suffrage Association leaflet, "Who Represents Her?" Another source was Jane Y. McCallum's chapter "Activities of Women in Texas Politics," in Frank Carter Adams, ed., *Texas Democracy: A Centennial History of Politics and Personalities of the Democratic Party 1836–1936*, vol. 1 (Austin: Democratic Historical Association, 1937). Other sources included: magazine articles by Mary Rider Lawrence, "Woman's Suffrage in Texas," *Texas Magazine*, vol. 6 (1912) and Lorraine Barnes, "Leader of the Petticoat Lobby," *The Texas Star*, 3 Oct. 1971; a book chapter, Sinclair Moreland, ed., "Jane Y. McCallum," *The Texas Women's Hall of Fame* (Austin: Biographical Press, 1917); newspaper articles by Lois Sager, "Petticoat Lobbyist Issues Some Tips," *Dallas Morning News*, 20 Jan. 1946; Barbara Karkabi, "Local Women Remember When They First Got the Vote," *Houston Chronicle*, 26 Aug. 1980; Gail Wolff, "Women Are People, Too: Battle-Cry 25 Years Ago," *Austin American-Statesman*, 16 Sept. 1945; Molly Connor Cook, "Fighting Suffragettes Suffered and Won Right to Vote During Hectic Days," *Austin American-Statesman*, 14 Nov. 1937. Additional sources included Willie D. Bowles, "The History of the Woman Suffrage Movement in Texas," (Thesis, The University of Texas at Austin, 1939); Ruthe Winegarten, "Brief Chronology of Woman Suffrage in Texas," (1979), unpublished paper in Texas Foundation for Women's Resources files, Austin; a letter from Minnie Fisher Cunningham to national suffrage leader Carrie Chapman Catt found in John C. Eudy's article, "The Vote and Lone Star Women: Minnie Fisher Cunningham and the Texas Equal Suffrage Association," *East Texas Historical Journal* vol. 14 (Fall, 1976).

Betty Jane McCallum, Austin

Jane Y. McCallum, circa 1892

Civil Rights Crusader — Christia Adair

The most extensive source for this story was a Christia Adair interview in the Black Oral History Project (1978), Schlesinger Library, Radcliffe College, Cambridge, Massachusetts; other sources included: Alicia Davis, "Christia V. Adair: A Servant of Humanity," *Texas Historian*, Sept. 1977; "And to Suffragist Christia Adair," *Daily Breakthrough*, 18 Nov. 1977; "The Drama of the Houston NAACP," *Forward Times*, 15 June 1959. Newspaper articles included: Rod Sallee "Mrs. C. V. Adair Link to Whites in Pioneering Rights," *Houston Chronicle*, 23 Oct. 1977; Karen Kane, "Over 70, I Don't Have Time to Get Old," *Houston Chronicle*, 15 Feb. 1978; Barbara Karkabi, "Christia Adair: Warrior, Winner," *Houston Chronicle*, 10 March 1980; Susan Caudill, "The Gracious Fighter," *Houston, Post*, 25 Feb. 1972. Another source was a pamphlet "Annual Houston NAACP Freedom Fund Dinner Souvenir Booklet," 22 Feb. 1980, in Mrs. Willie Lee Gay's files, Houston.

Christia Adair, left, with Mrs. Lyndon B. Johnson at the 1981 opening of the exhibit *Texas Women—A Celebration of History* in San Antonio.

Texas Foundation for Women's Resources

Texas Heroine: Cornelia Adair
Born: Geneseo, New York, 1838
Died: England, 1921
Most Notable Accomplishments: Co-founder of first ranch in Texas
   Panhandle, JA Ranch, 1877
   Sole owner of JA Ranch from 1885–1921
   Founder of Adair Hospital in Clarendon and the Clarendon
   YMCA, c. 1910s
Family Status: Married Montgomery Richie, 1857; widowed in 1864
   Married John Adair, British millionaire businessman, in 1869;
   widowed in 1885
   Mother of one son from first marriage
Personal Characteristics: Elegant, aristocratic, adventurous

Texas Heroine: Mary Ann "Molly" Goodnight
Born: Madison County, Tennessee, 1839
Died: Goodnight, Texas, 1926
Most Notable Accomplishments: Co-founder of first ranch in Texas
   Panhandle, JA Ranch, 1877
   Established and ran first home in Texas Panhandle, 1877
   Started first domestic buffalo herd, c. 1880s
   Founded Goodnight College, 1900
Family Status: Married Colonel Charles Goodnight, trail driver and
   cattle rancher, in 1870
   No children
Personal Characteristics: Resourceful, hospitable, gracious, known as
   "Mother of the Panhandle"

The Women of the JA Ranch — Cornelia Adair and Molly Goodnight

A source of information about the Goodnights was J. Evetts Haley's *Charles Goodnight: Cowman and Plainsman* (Boston and New York: Houghton Mifflin Co., 1936). Cornelia Adair's *My Diary, August 30 to November 5, 1874* (Austin: University of Texas Press, 1965) was the source for statements attributed to her. Additional sources were Pauline Durett Robertson and R. L. Robertson, *Panhandle Pilgrimage* (Amarillo, Tex.: Paramount Publishing Co., 1978); Laura V. Hamner's *The No-Gun Man of Texas: A Century of Achievement, 1835–1929* (Amarillo: Tex.: Laura Vernon Hamner, 1935) and *Short Grass and Longhorns* (Norman, Okla.: University of Oklahoma Press, 1943); and Harley True Burtons "History of the JA Ranch," (Thesis, The University of Texas at Austin, 1927).

WOMEN'S AIRFORCE SERVICE PILOTS

Program established: November 1942
Program dissolved: December 1944
Training Center: Avenger Field near Sweetwater, Texas
Director: Jacqueline Cochran
Qualifications: 35 flying hours
   High school graduate
   Between 18 and 34 years of age
   Excellent physical condition
Period of training: Six months
Number of WASP graduates: 1,074 (out of 25,000 applicants)
Number of WASPs who died in service: 38
Mission statistics: WASPs flew 60 million miles in 78 different types
   of military aircraft
   Ferried thousands of warplanes cross-country
   Towed targets for live gunnery practice
   Trained pilots, navigators and bombardiers
   Tested new and newly repaired aircraft

The Flying WASPs of World War II — WASPs

The main source for this story was a book by Sally Van Wegener Keil, *Those Wonderful Women in Their Flying Machines* (New York: Rawson, Wade, 1979). Another important source was an interview with Texas WASP Mildred Davidson Dalrymple by Janelle Scott, 1 Oct. 1981, and one with Texas WASP Colonel Betty Jane Williams by Frieda Werden, Spring 1981. Other sources included: Joan McCullough, *First of All* (New York: Holt, Rinehart and Winston, 1980); "Girl Pilots," *Life* vol. 15 (19 July 1943); Dudley Lynch, "A Flyby of Memories," in *Southwest Scene Magazine, Dallas Morning News,* 25 May 1974; Mary Brinkerhoff, "Former Flying Fifinellas See Years Fly By," *Dallas Morning News,* 18 June 1972; Sandra Glosser, "History Clips WASPs Wings," *Dallas Morning News,* 25 May 1974; "WASP, Women Airforce Service Pilots, World War II, 1980 Roster," in Texas Foundation for Women's Resources files, Austin.

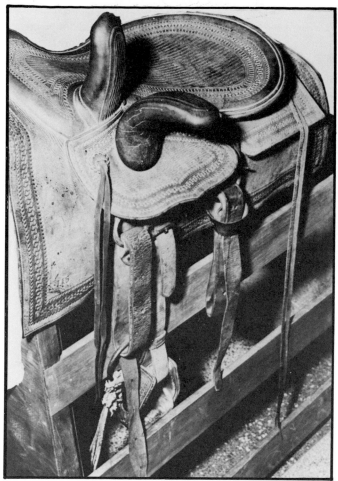

Below. Cornelia Adair, second from left, with a hunting party on the JA Ranch.
Left. Molly Goodnight's sidesaddle.

The flying WASPs, grounded by a West Texas snowstorm.

Astronauts Rhea Seddon, Kathryn Sullivan, Anna Fisher, Sally Ride and Judith Resnik.

NASA

SPACE WOMEN — AMERICA'S FIRST FEMALE ASTRONAUTS

Entry of women into astronaut corps:

> 1978 — First six women selected:
>> Anna L. Fisher, Physician
>> Shannon W. Lucid, Biochemist
>> Judith A. Resnik, Electrical Engineer
>> Sally K. Ride, Astrophysicist
>> Margaret Rhea Seddon, Surgeon
>> Kathryn D. Sullivan, Marine Geophysicist

> 1980 — Two additional women selected:
>> Mary L. Cleave, Sanitary Engineer
>> Bonnie J. Dunbar, Biomedical Engineer

Training Center: Lyndon B. Johnson Space Center, Houston, Texas

Qualifications: High intelligence
> Excellent physical condition
> Advanced technical and scientific knowledge
> Tolerance to extreme stress
> Flexibility and discipline

Period of Training: One year

Training activities: Undergoing the Air Force Survival Course in water and air
> Flying backseat in T-38 jet trainers 15 hours a month
> Flying in KC-135 high-altitude jets, whose parabolic flight patterns gives passengers 30 seconds of weightlessness
> Studying geology, astrophysics and orbital mechanics

Space Women —
America's First Female Astronauts

Sources for this story included several magazine articles: "Sextet for Space," *Newsweek* vol. 92, no. 7 (14 Aug. 1978); "NASA Picks Six Women Astronauts With the Message: You're Going A Long Way, Baby," *People* vol. 9, no. 5 (6 Feb. 1978); Lawrence Wright, "Space Cadet," *Texas Monthly* (July 1981); Susan Witty, "Our First Women in Space," *GEO* vol. 4, no. 9 (Sept. 1982). Facts about the U.S. space program were provided in "Manned Space Flight — The First Decade," *NASA Facts*, National Aeronautics and Space Administration, Lyndon B. Johnson Space Center, JSC 08062; "Space Benefits," *NASA Facts*, National Aeronautics and Space Administration, Lyndon B. Johnson Space Center, JSC 11626; "Space Shuttle," NASA Pamphlet, GPO: 1981, 0-347-862; and other NASA pamphlets. Sources for biographical data on each astronaut were NASA resumes. NASA is headquartered at the Lyndon B. Johnson Space Center in Houston, Texas.